Praise for L . Stephan Vincze
and *Inspiring Integrity*

When it comes to ensuring a healthy corporate culture—one that understands and respects the business value of compliance—Steve Vincze is the "go-to" professional. Steve and I have worked together in multiple companies to develop and instill a culture that can win with compliance at the forefront. This book is an essential read for those who want to do the right things in the right way. Winning with compliance is the only way to run your business.

Rich Daly
President and CEO, Catalyst Pharmaceuticals, Inc.

Steve Vincze has produced a gem of a book. Rather than looking at compliance as a burden, Steve sees it as a key to performance. Compliance officers and corporate leadership in general should read this book to understand how a compliance program can empower the entire company to do better.

Frank Lavin
Author of Export Now
Former US Ambassador

You would expect this book to be an excellent read for compliance officers and compliance professionals coming from a former chief compliance officer and US Marine. But what was unexpected is twofold: First, it's a tear jerker as we learn the compelling story of how leadership, honesty, and integrity were the backbone of Vincze's upbringing and the life of his family as immigrants from Hungary to the US. Second, this is not just a book for compliance officers and compliance professionals. It's a book for the C-suite and boards of directors that will inspire business executives to work with their compliance teams to do the right thing for their companies and for patients.

Meenakshi Datta
Partner, Sidley, Global Co-Leader Healthcare Practice
Global Life Sciences Leadership Council Member

I0030210

I have known Steve Vincze as a passionate ethics and compliance pioneer for twenty-five years. We first met in Washington in 1999 at the very first Pharmaceutical and Medical Device Ethics & Compliance Congress, where Steve was the first speaker ever to present on international compliance, presenting his International LL.M. thesis from Georgetown Law School. Steve rose to prominence in the ethics and compliance profession in the early 2000s as a result of his leadership and cutting-edge innovations in branding, training, monitoring, and measuring compliance program effectiveness while implementing what was at the time the largest corporate settlement agreement (CIA) in the history of the pharmaceutical industry at TAP Pharmaceuticals.

From Washington to Budapest to Istanbul, I have invited Steve over the years to share his uniquely creative, business-friendly, and practical compliance wisdom. An excellent and engaging presenter, you can count on Steve to weave in historical references, present engaging graphics, and keep it fun with his dry, self-deprecating wit, while at the same time reminding us how to apply tough but effective leadership standards he learned as a proud Marine Corps officer.

So it comes as no surprise that his new book, *Inspiring Integrity: How to Win with Compliance and Propel Performance*, does exactly the same thing—only better! What was a surprise is just how moving some portions of the book are. Packed full of colorful anecdotes, practical advice, and useful checklists, this truly is a wonderful book for both practitioners in the trenches and theorists in the classroom. It is an absolute *must read* for all C-suite executives, board members, and business, legal, and compliance leaders. Always inspiring about compliance in person, Steve has re-inspired me with his book. Read *Inspiring Integrity*—I guarantee you will be inspired too!

Peter N. Grant, JD, PhD
President and CEO, Health Care Conference Administrators, LLC (dba Global Health Care, LLC), Senior Advisor and Former Chair, Health Law Section, Davis Wright Tremaine, and Chair of Health Policy Publishing, LLC
Advisory Board Member, Harvard Health Policy Review
Former member, editorial board of Health Affairs

Wow. This is an important book. *Inspiring Integrity* is not just about compliance; it's about how to develop a culture based on ethics and integrity, which every organization needs. Every CEO and director should read and draw inspiration from it.

Michael Gibbs
Clinical Professor of Economics,
University of Chicago Booth School of Business

Steve Vincze's pathbreaking book is worth an entire degree program in corporate compliance. He writes movingly about the challenge of leading leaders to embrace and embody the virtues of inspiration, integrity, ethics, and compliance. The health care industry desperately needs to rediscover its bearings, and there's no better place to start than this insightful volume. Beyond health care, every industry or business, large or small, will benefit from the author's decades of experience and wisdom.

Thomas Wm. Mayo
Professor of Law & Altshuler University,
Distinguished Teaching Professor
Professor (adj.), Department of Internal Medicine,
UT-Southwestern Medical School
of Counsel, Haynes Boone, LLP., SMU/Dedman School of Law

I have long observed that the most effective professionals have one foot in the library and one foot in the street. That is, they allow theory to inform practice, and practice to inform theory. Given that Steve Vincze has spent a decorated career toggling between those two venues, it comes as no surprise that *Inspiring Integrity* is both compelling and illuminating. The book offers a fresh perspective from which to view compliance and, as such, is required reading for both emerging and existing leaders.

David A. Shore
Former Associate Dean and current Faculty, Harvard University
Former Distinguished Professor of Innovation and Change, Tianjin University of
Finance and Economics (China)

L. Stephan Vincze's *Inspiring Integrity* is an ethics and compliance toolkit and treatise as to the "why" ethics and compliance are critically important in our ever-evolving world of risk and opportunity. Combining his personal and professional experiences, Mr. Vincze maps out how we can drive ethical outcomes and sustainable decisions through structures, messaging, and leadership. The book is a road map on how to create and sustain ethics and integrity in an organization, as well as how compliant practices can be an instrumental partner to commercial success. It is a book about how values don't come to life on fancy wall posters, aspirational values, and intranet messages, but how they come to life through our decisions and decision-making. While "just say no" to unethical practices might sound nice and easy, Mr. Vincze guides us as to how we can operationalize those messages so they are calibrated to the real-world risks that people, teams, and organizations face in their work and roles.

Although Mr. Vincze's background is in life-sciences, I would recommend this book to anyone working in ethics and compliance, including those who are just starting, or considering a career in business integrity. Mr. Vincze demonstrates through his career journey how policies, rules, and procedures are not there to slow anyone down, but to help everyone appreciate that they, as an individual and a team, are the guardians and gatekeepers to corporate integrity and values.

In sum, this is an inspiring and heartfelt book on leadership, purpose, values, mission, and trust, and how they are all instrumental to a "best in class" ethical and compliant organization.

Richard Bistrong,
CEO, Front-Line Anti-Bribery LLC

Reading *Inspiring Integrity: How to Win with Compliance and Propel Performance* has been a transformative experience. The author eloquently argues that ethical leadership and a culture of integrity are not just regulatory necessities but pivotal drivers of organizational success and personal moral growth. Through compelling narratives and stripped of pedantic education, this book addresses ethics and compliance, illustrating their importance in motivating leaders to redefine the role of compliance in business, demonstrating how adherence to core values and human dignity can drive innovation and performance. The book enthralls you through a genuine narrative, enriched by the author's personal experience, emphasizing the importance of human dignity, ethical leadership, and the emotional connection needed to inspire integrity and actions for long-term success and (personal) human flourishing.

Ruggero Gramatica, PhD
CEO, Macrocosm Group Honorary Research Associate,
The Oxford University Institute for New Economic Thinking Investment Advisory

Inspiring Integrity, by Steve Vincze, is a revelation for CEOs and board members who are responsible for the success of any kind of organization. The author makes a compelling case that as leaders pursue their business objectives, it should be done with ethics and compliance as core values. Many CEOs and board members think compliance is just a legal checklist of policies and procedures to avoid regulatory problems. The book explains that it is better to inspire all people in the enterprise to want to comply not for compliance's sake but in pursuit of a greater good. Mr. Vincze explains it is vitally important to integrate your company values and principles to form a culture of compliance.

This is valuable learning for C-suite executives, board members, and shareholders alike.

Rick LeBlanc, BASc (EE), MBA
Operating Partner, Huron Capital Partner
Seasoned CEO and Board Member of companies up to $2B

Pharmaceuticals is one the most sophisticated industries. As such, pharmaceutical development comes with complexity, norms, standards, facts, and data. When a product is approved and commercial activities start, similar rigor must be applied forward. In other words, integrity and compliance with codes of conduct throughout activities must prevail.

Could strong values and ethics enable business innovation, growth, and sustainability? Absolutely! Why? Because integrity is about respect for all of our stakeholders: payors, health care professional, patients, and shareholders. Lack of integrity could lead to serious reputational damage and broader harm. Consequences as severe as deaths can be at the end of the line.

In the pharmaceutical industry, we all carry the same mission: to improve the lives of patients. We create expectations and hope, and as such our principles all the way through research, development, and commercialization activities cannot be compromised.

Make this a personal commitment throughout your entire career and you'll be proud the day you look back.

Anyone working in the pharmaceutical industry, directly or indirectly, would benefit from reading *Inspiring Integrity* by Steve Vincze for insights on the role integrity plays both at a high level but also in the day-to-day activities.

Paul Levesque
President & CEO, Theratechnologies

Inspiring Integrity is special because Steve Vincze is special. The "how to do compliance right" content is full of practical tips and important insights. These come to life through Steve's eyes as he weaves stories from his professional and personal life into a compelling, and often moving, reflection on what it takes to sustain a winning performance.

Steve Priest
President, Integrity Insight International

Steve Vincze is the best at what he does! For nearly thirty years, Steve has inspired greatness by making compliance a force multiplier for the life sciences industry. He does this by "living and breathing" the value that integrity brings to each and every organization from the CEO to those in the trenches interacting with patients on a daily basis. Steve has undoubtedly written *the* playbook for success!

Kathleen Coffey
Experienced CEO and Board Member

Inspired by amazing chapters of his own life journey and shaped by his life sciences background, L. Stephan Vincze is offering astonishing compliance principles for modern progressive companies and their leadership. Essential takeaways are driven by his deep competence and experience in the compliance field, including highest ethics and integrity standards. An absolute must-read guide for leadership suite, management, and entrepreneurs.

Dr. Volker E. Kuebler, MBA
Experienced CEO and Senior Business Executive

Inspiring Integrity is about more than compliance; it's about doing things right, leadership, and improving performance for successful organizations.

I learned about the significance of compliance as a young executive. We were a fast-growing, publicly traded healthcare company, and one of my first meetings as a recently promoted VP was about compliance. Our CEO, noticing my lack of interest in the topic, took me aside and said that great companies do all things great, and that it starts with compliance. From that day, with companies I have led, and public and private company boards that I have been on, I support a disciplined, thorough compliance program. If you're going to do something, do it right. As Steve points out, at its foundation, that's compliance.

I also enjoyed this book because I learned even more about Steve. His younger years, through his education, to his time in the Corps, and his successful corporate and family life. Steve's a driven, smart, passionate, and hugely proud American.

Show me a company with a strong compliance program and I'll show you a company that most likely does everything right. That's the company you want to be part of, that's the company you want to lead, that's the company you want to invest in. Read the book.

James T. Barry
CEO, Celerity05

I have been working with Steve Vincze and TRESTLE Compliance for over two years in connection with the commercialization of our products in the United States. Steve and TRESTLE have played an important role in shaping our compliance department, providing sound and practical advice whenever they were asked to. Their professionalism is outstanding and we are glad to have partnered with Steve and TRESTLE for our compliance needs.

Inspiring Integrity is a book that should be read by every leader who has ethics and integrity at heart and who is in a position to make a change in cultural behavior within their organization.

Jocelyn Lafond, LL.B., LL.M.
General Counsel and Corporate Secretary, Theratechnologies

Who better to take lessons from in compliance than Steve Vincze? Steve has built a career and business on the cornerstones of ethics and integrity. Steve was an early adopter of compliance and its key components early in his personal and professional lives. Let Steve's story and lessons be motivating factors behind your personal, professional, and industrial compliance efforts. In *Inspiring Integrity: How to Win With Compliance and Propel Performance* readers will undoubtedly find motivation in Steve's compliance anecdotes, lessons, and examples.

Tyler Wiseman

Chief Legal Officer, Elevar Therapeutics

Inspiring Integrity: How to Win with Compliance and Propel Performance may as well be called the eighth element of an effective ethics and compliance program. It is an essential read for ethics and compliance professionals and senior executives, generally. It is a manual for compelling ethical conduct delivered within an engaging story born of Steve's upbringing and diverse career achievements. Those of us responsible for conceiving organizational strategy and implementing that strategy from all seniority will identify with and benefit from Steve's leadership philosophy and tactical recommendations. Reading about Steve's experiences in government service and as a pioneer in the ethics and compliance profession will orient you to the history that shaped current public policy, empower you to hold the line against well-known forms of misconduct, and adapt to the emerging ethical challenges and regulatory expectations facing all industries. I have been fortunate to witness Steve apply these principles directly as a colleague and subsequently as a client. I highly recommend this book to those looking to make a values-driven impact on their own organization or broader community.

Gerard Leeman

Senior Director, Compliance ONO PHARMA USA, Inc.

I have known Steve for almost forty years, and he has been a paragon of character and competence in every position he has held. This book stresses the fact that compliance, trust, and integrity must be present within any organization if success is to be achieved. Trust both inside the organization among employees and leadership and outside the organization with clients and customers is cemented by a well-crafted compliance program. Execution of the compliance program must be driven by a corporate leadership culture of trust and integrity. Steve's book provides a vital roadmap to ensuring compliance is a way of life and an uncompromising standard, instead of an afterthought viewed as an inconvenience.

John F. Sattler

Lt. General, USMC (Ret.); former Director of Strategic Plans and Policy, U.S. Joint Chiefs of Staff; former United States' representative to the Military Staff Committee of the United Nations; former Distinguished Chair of Leadership at the Stockdale Center for Ethical Leadership, United States Naval Academy

INSPIRING
INTEGRITY

HOW TO WIN WITH COMPLIANCE
AND PROPEL PERFORMANCE

L. STEPHAN VINCZE

Advantage | Books

Published by Advantage Books, Charleston, South Carolina.
An imprint of Advantage Media.

ADVANTAGE is a registered trademark, and the Advantage colophon is a trademark of Advantage Media Group, Inc.

Printed in the United States of America.

10 9 8 7 6 5 4 3 2 1

ISBN: 979-8-89188-206-5 (Hardcover)
ISBN: 978-1-64225-556-0 (Paperback)
ISBN: 978-1-64225-555-3 (eBook)

Library of Congress Control Number: 2024918093

Book design by Wesley Strickland.

This publication is designed to provide accurate and authoritative information in regard to the subject matter covered. It is sold with the understanding that the publisher is not engaged in rendering legal, accounting, or other professional services. If legal advice or other expert assistance is required, the services of a competent professional person should be sought.

Advantage Books is an imprint of Advantage Media Group. Advantage Media helps busy entrepreneurs, CEOs, and leaders write and publish a book to grow their business and become the authority in their field. Advantage authors comprise an exclusive community of industry professionals, idea-makers, and thought leaders. For more information go to **advantagemedia.com**.

To my beloved daughter, Chiara,

I dedicate this book to you. You have inspired me every day of your life. You inspired me to fight for my life, to kick COVID's butt, and to live for you. You inspired me to write this book. You are my gift from God. You have inspired me to be selfless.

May this book inspire you, and others, to be people of integrity and people of strength. If it does, I know you will be confident, happy, and successful. Remember to enjoy your life. Have fun living it to the fullest!

With all my love, your proud father,

Dad

CONTENTS

ACKNOWLEDGMENTS

This book is the product of years of hard work, support, and, yes, inspiration from many, many people. While I can't possibly name everyone, let me thank and acknowledge the following:

My family, whose love, support, and leadership by example throughout my life helped make me the man that I am.

My teachers and professors, who taught me the love of learning and the need to stay intellectually curious throughout one's life.

My coaches and teammates, who instilled in me the importance of competing against an inner standard of physical excellence to persevere and to never, ever give up.

My Marine Corps leaders, commanding officers, and troops, who showed me the meaning and value of *esprit de corps* and what it takes to accomplish a mission, any mission.

My legal mentors and colleagues, who inspired me with their intellectual rigor and dedication to the rule of law.

My political mentors and colleagues in Washington, who refreshingly gave me confidence that there are indeed very competent and patriotic people who serve the American people in our government.

My consulting mentors and colleagues, who taught me the importance of "walking in your client's shoes" and the value of listening before speaking.

My corporate leaders and colleagues, who demonstrated to me that financial success results from a combination of thoughtful, sincere, and genuine human leadership combined with precise execution of well-thought-out strategic and tactical plans.

My TRESTLE Compliance Team and Advisory Board, whose support, expertise, intellect, and shared dedication to excellence have created a culture of continuous curiosity, client service, and professional excellence in our firm.

My clients, who have entrusted me and my firm to provide solutions to their corporate, compliance, and privacy needs and challenges, whose trust I will forever honor and value, and who have shown that there is indeed integrity in the life sciences industry.

My doctors and nurses, who saved my life from COVID-19 and whose professionalism and courage demonstrated that they are the true heroes of our age.

My publisher, Advantage/Forbes Books, whose editorial, cover design, marketing, and media relations teams made the writing of this book and the sharing of my story with a national and global audience possible.

To everyone, Thank You!

L. Stephan Vincze ("Steve")

My family: Me with my wonderful wife, Kathy, and my precious daughter, Chiara.

AT THE CORNER OF ETHICS AND INTEGRITY

Educating the mind without educating the heart is no education at all.

—ARISTOTLE

When I say the word "compliance," I think most people imagine a doorstop of a manual full of legalese in fine print. They likely roll their eyes and cringe at the thought. The words "dry," "boring," "onerous," and even "scary" come to mind. For those in life sciences—biotech, pharmaceuticals, and medical device companies—they may think of the compliance officers and consultants as those picky, pesky people driving them crazy with regulations, policies, forms, and documentation and, yes, with dry, boring, endless training.

I am one of those picky, pesky people—except that there is so much more to compliance. For me, compliance has become a passion. My job is to help the companies I work with realize that compliance can be, and indeed *should be*, so much more. If practiced properly, it can be a source of inspiration, motivation, and a true business force multiplier—in short, a competitive advantage that propels performance.

Compliance lives at the corner of ethics and integrity.

Ethics and values, far more than a book of compliance regulations, tend to get most people's attention. But just in case, I like to ensure we make it memorable by touching peoples' hearts and minds. Perhaps the most memorable example we captured was in a video we produced for a national sales meeting for one of our clients.

The real-life family who volunteered for this video had a young son with a very rare, debilitating disease. Our client had created a medical therapy that helped children with a different form of that disease. But this family's son had a rarer form of this life-threatening disease, and the company was still conducting research to try to address this ultra-rare type. As the video came to its conclusion, after introducing the family and their son, the mother of this ill little boy looked straight into the camera and pleaded, "I want you sales folks to stay compliant, and here's why … You've met my son. He's a very, very sick little boy. We're counting on your company to continue the research to find a cure for him, which currently doesn't exist. And without a cure, he and other kids like him are going to die." She paused, then continued, staring directly into the camera. "He will die. This is a matter of life and death. So when you're out there in the field, remember my son. I ask you to be compliant so that your company doesn't go through an investigation that costs millions of dollars that could jeopardize my son's life. It really comes down to that. Be compliant for my son, be compliant for other kids like him, because what you do out there really matters. What you do out there can affect the lives of these kids."

This spontaneous, heartfelt plea from a loving mother moved everyone in the audience. The entire sales force stood up and gave a standing ovation. That's the kind of inspiration and motivation that touches both hearts and minds that needs to be part of compliance. That's what I mean by "inspiring integrity" and "winning with compliance and propelling performance."

There's a similar story with Robert Coughlin, a well-known leader in the biotech industry, who was the president and CEO of MassBio, which helped attract pharmaceutical investment into Boston to the point where it is now the recognized global hub of biotech. He was motivated by his son Bobby, who was born with cystic fibrosis.[1] His son was diagnosed in utero, enabling cutting-edge treatments—and Bob Coughlin left no stone unturned in trying to help his child. Today, his son is a healthy, strapping young man, thanks to Bob's unyielding passion to find a therapy for his son and the miracles of science and the biotech industry.

Similarly, Biotech CEO Brad Thompson wrote how his mother's death from lung cancer impacted him and his choice in focusing on cancer treatments.[2]

In biotech, medicine, research, and development, we get to witness these scientific miracles. Things our parents' generation could only dream of are now reality. These miracles are in and of themselves inspiring. But our challenges remain.

I am there to get my clients across the finish line, whether that is in launching a new product, enabling a successful M&A transaction, responding to an investigation, or implementing a settlement agreement. How do I get my clients to be as excited about compliance as I am? It starts with remembering that compliance resides at

---

1   "Bob Coughlin: Boldly Chasing Cures," Know Rare, accessed September 27, 2023, https://knowrare.com/blog-v2/bob-coughlin.

2   Brad Thompson, "How an Executive's Health Challenges Can Make a Biotech Stronger," *Life Science Leader,* February 25, 2015, https://www.lifescienceleader.com/doc/how-an-executive-s-health-challenges-can-make-a-biotech-stronger-0001.

that corner of ethics and integrity. Behind the Excel sheets and lab reports and the millions of numbers run through many algorithms and computers, behind the sales and corporate progress, behind the new artificial intelligence entering all industries, behind it all are *people*—the employees and colleagues at firms trying to cure diseases and make life better for all, the people of all ages and backgrounds who suffer from various diseases and conditions, and all their loved ones and those around them who are impacted too.

For me, it all starts with a sense of integrity and ethics, a set of core values that guide our thoughts and actions, that include empathy to our fellow human beings, as well as honesty and trustworthiness. Ethics and integrity, truth and honesty, don't just exist in the abstract as higher guiding principles. As a practical matter, practicing and living these values is what creates trust—trust with people and trust with companies that you want to do business with, to have a relationship with. Trust is the glue that makes compliance and business success possible.

Where It Began

You bring your ethics and integrity with you to whatever position you hold. I've been in the field of healthcare and life sciences compliance for over twenty-five years, and before that I served as an officer in the United States Marines.

But I learned ethics and honesty as a boy—and I learned it at home.

My dad was very strict and "old school." He definitely had expectations for me as the oldest son of two Hungarian immigrants. He wanted me to follow in his footsteps and become a physician. My mother, while also quite strict with high expectations, was different.

While my dad focused on academics (anything less than an A was unacceptable), she focused on sports, proper dress, manners, and appreciation for the arts and culture. She always believed in me, saying in her thick Hungarian accent, "You can do it! Never give up. Always try your best. Remember, it can always be worse. You can be whatever you want to be." By contrast, candidly, my father never seemed to believe in me, at least outwardly. It was only many years later that I realized, in his "tough love" kind of way, why my father was so hard on me. He expected the best from me precisely because he believed I was capable of it. He just didn't express it very well.

One thing, however, that I knew about my father, both as a doctor and as a man, was his honesty and integrity. One of the clearest lessons on that was when I was about eighteen and working in the hospital where my father was chairman of the OB-GYN department. My family believed that nothing is given to you. You have to earn everything. Thus, when I asked for an allowance at the age of seven, they asked me what I would do to earn it! So I cut grass, shoveled snow, and shined shoes. Fast-forward eleven years, and I was pretty full of myself as an eighteen-year-old preppy Andover grad, Ivy Leaguer, recruited to Columbia for rowing, and finishing up my freshman year on the dean's list as a premed student. Yet in my family, you still start at the bottom to learn the life lesson that if you don't work hard, that's exactly where you may end up! So I found myself mopping floors on a surgical ICU floor as my summer job.

My dad, Laszlo O. Vincze, MD (Dr. LOV), and my mom, Marianne Szent-Ivanyi Magyar Vincze, June 2001

Life's lessons are best learned by living life. Witnessing firsthand healthcare professionals (HCPs) in action with sick patients was an eye-opening education for me. For one, I realized how much I did not like being around all the blood and guts and the nitty-gritty of sick people. And guess what—on a surgical ICU floor, there was a lot of it for me to mop up daily! I know that sounds terrible, but it was (and still is) the truth. I definitely did not have the stomach to be a doctor! (My wife still laughs out loud at the thought.) Just as importantly, however, I realized how dedicated and special these HCPs were, and that included, most especially, my father. I witnessed my father's compassion and his competence as a physician; he truly cared about his patients. Each patient or family member he spoke to was treated as if their case were the most important in the world, and he spoke gently but knowledgeably, invoking confidence in his care.

Moreover, the hospital staff loved him. They would share, "Are you Dr. Vincze's son? He's a wonderful doctor. You should be very proud." Powerfully, I saw a whole new side of my father, the professional side and how he combined his hard work and exceptional medical training with his true caring and empathy for people. He was indeed a very good man. At the time, however, as an obnoxious eighteen-year-old, I just thought, "He sure is a lot nicer in the hospital with other people than he is with me at home!" Someday, perhaps, when my now-thirteen-year-old daughter reads this, she may think something similar of me!

Fast-forward nearly forty years to 2017. I was awakened at midnight and told that my father was in the emergency room at Mount Auburn Hospital in Cambridge with a severe case of pneumonia. As we learned later, he had also suffered a stroke. Living in the Back Bay in downtown Boston, I was the closest relative to the hospital, so of course, I raced to get to him as quickly as I could.

The ER nurse came out, greeted me, and asked, "Are you Dr. Vincze's son?"

I answered, "Yes, I am."

Then she said, "Is this by any chance the same Dr. Vincze from Melrose?"

I told her, "Yes, that's him, but he now lives in Charlestown."

She then paused, smiled, and shared that thirty-five years before, he had delivered her first child, her eldest son. With a tinge of sadness, as she knew my father was very sick, she added, "You should know, he was the best doctor I ever had."

A few months later, now in a nursing home and under hospice care, my father's hospice nurse pulled me aside and said that my father had been her physician many years ago as well. Her words echoed those of the other nurse: "He was the best doctor I ever had."

Clearly, my father's dedication and sincere caring for his patients had left lifelong impressions. He made a positive difference in the lives of his patients … and, ultimately, in mine. He combined his professional skill and knowledge with his human compassion and genuine caring for the people who trusted him with their health and well-being.

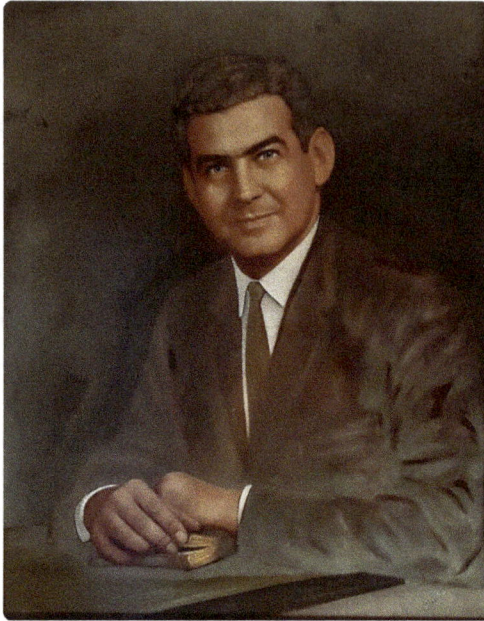

Laszlo O. Vincze, MD

In writing this book and reflecting on my life's journey, I have realized the common thread throughout my life has been trying to live the values instilled in me by my parents—values I carry with me to this day in my role in compliance and how important that is.

As a premed freshman at Columbia and stroke of the first boat of the Columbia freshman crew team, I was a cocky, some might say even arrogant, kid who thought he had the world completely figured out. Fast-forward forty-plus years, four degrees later, service as a United States Marine Corps officer, a career in law, consulting, and compliance, surviving COVID-19, and most importantly, being a dad and husband, my life has taught me just how little I knew back then—and how much I'm still learning! Physical and mental strength, with which I was blessed as a young man, are not the only strengths that matter. Humility, empathy, and kindness, combined with vision, wisdom, and the confidence to act in the face of uncertainty and fear, are the mature strengths that experienced leaders exercise to inspire and motivate others to act and commit to a purpose greater than themselves. I learned this both at home, in the Marines, and as a leader in my chosen career. Those who lose sight of their values inevitably lose their way.

Perhaps the number one question compliance officers ponder is this:

How do you get people to want to comply?

The answer in a word is leadership.

> *My definition of a leader in a free country is a man*
> *who can persuade people to do what they don't want to*
> *do, or do what they're too lazy to do, and like it.*
>
> **—PRES. HARRY TRUMAN**

More specifically, the answer is to win the trust and respect of people by connecting to their hearts and minds. You do this by inspiring them to a purpose greater than themselves. You must learn to see the world through the eyes of your audience, to understand their challenges, their obstacles, their fears … and their motivations. Only then, when you speak the truth and answer the question, "Why should you comply?" will they listen to, understand, and embrace your advice. Character counts, as do consequences. You must be tough. And you must instill in them the importance—and in the life sciences, the real meaning of life-and-death discoveries and research—of compliance.

Win hearts and minds to win respect. That's what my father did. That is what I try to do.

1976 Columbia Freshman Lightweight Crew First Boat: That's me at the end, on the far right, number eight from left to right, the stroke of the boat.

One important substantive addition: To keep trust and respect, once won, you must deliver results. With pain, there better be gain! No tough coach lasts long without wins. On a more superficial level, looking back, I envy the eighteen-year-old version of me—for the hair—I really miss the hair!

Living Compliance

I want to help readers of this book—those in the C-suite, the boardroom, and others in the life sciences, as well as in other industries, and students in law schools and business schools who aspire to those levels—to see compliance not as an onerous chore but as a force multiplier that reinforces the importance of character and integrity, that ensures fiscal responsibility, and that demonstrates a commitment to health and safety, from which stem business and financial success. Your compliance program, whether you are building it from the ground up or updating an existing one, is the foundation for answering the questions, "What kind of business are we? Who *are* we? What do we represent?" Driven by values and principles, a compliance program is a vehicle to define your business and live it day-to-day.

Commitment to integrity and compliance ensures your reputational capital not only remains intact but also grows. And like a magnet, that capital will attract and keep talent, as people want to work for companies they respect. They want to be proud of their company. Reputation matters. In fact, a nationwide survey of fifteen hundred people concluded that a nudge over 83 percent of them consider reputation and alignment with personal views more important than a higher salary.[3] When businesses speak of employee engagement, that kind of weight on reputation shows how important it is to those who work with you.

Of course, compliance is a liability prevention tool as well—a form of insurance, if you will—to protect you when bad things happen. Audits and lawsuits are expensive propositions.

Ultimately, though, a compliance program is an extension of your company's commitment to ethics and integrity. To briefly define them:

Ethics: The principles, beliefs, morals, and values someone espouses.

Integrity: How someone applies and *lives* their ethics out in the real world.

Investing in a quality ethics and compliance program is about doing *more* than what is required.

---

3   "Employees Consider Company's Reputation, Alignment with Their Own Views More Important Than Higher Salary," Success Communications Group, October 21, 2021, https://www.globenewswire.com/en/news-release/2021/10/21/2318546/0/en/Poll-Employees-consider-company-s-reputation-alignment-with-their-own-views-more-important-than-higher-salary.html.

Compliance is about doing what's right, not just what's required.

When I come into a company, I'm often thought of as simply "the compliance guy." At first, people are less than thrilled to see "the compliance guy." Frankly, the standard reaction from people who do not know me but only know what I do is, "Oh shit!" To the uninformed, compliance is often thought of as nothing but a myriad of rules and cumbersome administrative requirements. Scientists and people in the life sciences industry, however, by definition, seek new discoveries, breaking boundaries in the process, exploring and experimenting in unknown areas of human medical knowledge, to be on the cutting edges of science and discovery. People in the life sciences are inherently innovators who don't accept the status quo and current "rules." They don't want to play by the rules per se—they want to discover and define new ones. I get it. It's in our American culture, our heritage, our DNA, if you will, as innovators born out of a revolution. And that's the way it needs to be and should be for the industry to continue to cure and treat diseases. It is in this inspiring and motivating environment that as both a legal and practical matter, we must practically and effectively insert "ethics and compliance."

In this context, I find it extremely gratifying when I can help passionate life sciences executives and employees create a thriving corporate culture with a compliance program that supports their quest for innovation and new discoveries—one that fills them with confidence—a confidence derived from the assurance that an effective compliance program enables them to be both aggressive *and* compliant.

My years of professional experience have positioned me to share my unique knowledge and insights through this practical, actionable book. My goal is that this book will be of help to CEOs, board members, general counsels (GCs), chief operating officers (COOs), chief compliance officers, and privacy officers, as well as to aspiring lawyers/law students, business school students, and venture capitalists/investors. It is intended for anyone who needs an easy-to-understand, comprehensive, practical, yet authoritative guide on compliance programs generally and life science commercial compliance programs specifically—and how to make them work.

It is my hope that my passion for this topic will leap from the page and inspire readers. I invite you to share in this passion for compliance in the spirit of making your company great. Let's begin!

CHAPTER 1:

THE ROLE OF LEADERSHIP: TO INSPIRE AND MOTIVATE

If your actions inspire others to dream more, learn more,
do more and become more, you are a leader.

—JOHN QUINCY ADAMS

A
s an officer in the Marine Corps, I learned early on that no matter how high you rise up the ranks, the best leaders are those who lead by example. Getting out from behind their desk and into the field, they endure the rain, snow, hot desert sun, or whatever Mother Nature throws at them or their fellow Marines. Physically seeing, experiencing, and feeling what each Marine encounters is worth its weight in gold.

As an executive or compliance professional, you, or the right representative, need to get out into the field as well.

When it comes to understanding and supporting your sales force or workforce, knowing the challenges they experience firsthand builds credibility, respect, and trust. They know you are not off in an "ivory tower" but understand what is happening in the trenches as well.

This will enable you to better understand their challenges and better support and arm them with the tools to compete and win aggressively while safely in compliance.

As I mentioned in the introduction, "compliance" tends to be a word that fills many with anxiety or even irritation. As with most things, the right leadership and tone can make all the difference. This chapter will show how leading by example can turn compliance into a competitive advantage.

Yes, that's me in the middle: 1st Lt. L. S. Vincze, USMC, in the field with E Battery, Second Battalion, Eleventh Marines, First Marine Division, 1984.

Create a Culture of Compliance

Enron, Tyco, Theranos, FTX … when there is not a culture of ethics, integrity, and, yes, compliance, the fallout can be dramatic and stunning. Names like those make headlines—and most companies never recover. (Not to mention those involved often find themselves staring down federal agents.)

Compliance should permeate your entire company beginning with the president, CEO, chief financial officer, and the board of directors. It must be rooted in the consciousness of every person from the shop floor to the executive suite and boardroom. *It must be a part of your corporate DNA.* Compliance is one area where a driven process, from the top to the bottom, is critical. The compliance officer is the person responsible for implementing a compliance program that is established by top management and corporate owners and overseen by the board of directors.

All positions in a company, whether it is in manufacturing, sales, marketing, or R&D, must work together to support compliance goals. It takes everyone in the company to understand the compliance aspect of their operation and the risk of potential regulatory violations—and resulting flameouts and PR disasters, not to mention the human toll. In other words compliance is something that everyone in the company must live, day in and day out. Leaving it up to the compliance officer alone to establish the guidelines and ethics to carry the entire company is an accident waiting to happen.

THE THERANOS CASE—"FAKE IT TILL YOU MAKE IT"

One of the most notable examples of issues of ethics and integrity involves Elizabeth Holmes, the founder of Theranos, who claimed to develop a unique blood-testing device that revolutionized the process of drawing blood in clinical labs. She founded her company at the age of nineteen, and by 2014 it had a valuation of $9 billion. Hailed as a genius, she became the youngest female self-made billionaire in the world.[4]

Unfortunately, it all came crashing down when Theranos's technology was exposed as bogus, with inaccuracies and various shortcomings, which Holmes covered up. It wasn't long before she was ousted as CEO and charged with massive fraud, forcing the company to close its testing centers and labs, shutting down their operations completely. Convicted, she is currently serving an eleven-and-a-half-year sentence in federal prison.[5]

The Theranos case study is a perfect example of how a passionate visionary, very bright founder, and leader lost sight of reality and was set on overcoming adversity. Her company wasn't grounded in ethical core values or principles. As a leader, she should have taken different steps from a compliance perspective that could have resolved the problems that arose. For example, Walgreen investors were not allowed in the lab to examine the data, employees worked in silos and were not allowed to share information with each other, and engineers modified standard testing machines to make them look like Theranos's new minilabs and passed off third-party testers as their own.[6] Her COO, with whom she was at one point romantically involved, Sunny Balwani, also drew a prison sentence for his role in this disaster. This is a case too where *someone* should have been challenging leader-

---

4   Daniel Thomas, "Theranos Scandal: Who Is Elizabeth Holmes and Why Was She on Trial?," bbc. com, November 19, 2022, https://www.bbc.com/news/business-58336998.

5   Bobby Allyn, "Elizabeth Holmes Has Started Her 11-Year Prison Sentence. Here's What to Know," NPR, updated May 30, 2023, https://www.npr.org/2023/05/30/1178728092/ elizabeth-holmes-prison-sentence-theranos-fraud-silicon-valley.

6   "Elizabeth Holmes and the Theranos Case: History of a Fraud Scandal," Integrity Line, updated November 22, 2023, https://www.integrityline.com/expertise/blog/elizabeth-holmes-theranos/#:~:text=Through%20whistleblower%20revelations%20and%20the,handle%20 were%20flawed%20and%20unreliable.

ship—they should have been challenging each other—and yet they went along with the scheme together. All of these issues could have been addressed and not covered up if a compliance program were in place from the beginning.

FTX

Sam Bankman-Fried, at the time of sentencing just thirty-two years old, was sent to prison for twenty-five years for fraud related to his company FTX, a cryptocurrency exchange. The judge in the case, when sentencing Bankman-Fried, said he had an "extreme appetite for risk."[7] At one time the exchange, based in the Bahamas, had a $30 billion valuation.[8] However, a run on deposits exposed the fact that Bankman-Fried was "looting" his own company as a piggy bank.[9]

A *Financial Times* article claimed, "[T]he trial … cast a harsh light on reckless borrowing, risk-taking and handling of customer money within the crypto industry at the height of the 2022 bubble, as creditors now seek to recoup billions of dollars in several high-profile bankruptcies and US regulators battle with other big crypto companies, including the largest exchange, Binance."[10]

Bankman-Fried spent his ill-gotten gains writing big checks to political candidates and buying sports teams and real estate.[11] Bankman-Fried and Elizabeth Holmes are both cautionary tales where very

---

7 David Yaffe-Bellany and J. Edward Moreno, "Sam Bankman-Fried Sentenced to 25 Years in Prison," nytimes.com, March 28, 2024, https://www.nytimes.com/2024/03/28/technology/sam-bankman-fried-sentenced.html.

8 Ibid.

9 Ibid.

10 "FTX Founder Sam Bankman-Fried Prepares for the Fight of His Life in US Trial," ft.com, October 1, 2023, https://www.ft.com/content/a42c7421-fc9e-40ae-a76a-f81334ed4749.

11 Lakshmi Varanasi, "Sam Bankman-Fried Spent a Fortune. Now, Lawyers Say 'the Emperor Had No Clothes.' Here's Where the Money Went," Business Insider, November 23, 2022, https://www.businessinsider.com/how-ftxs-sam-bankman-fried-allegedly-spent-his-fortune-2022-11#:~:text=At%20his%20peak%2C%20Sam%20Bankman,donations%2C%20and%20funding%20sports%20teams.

intelligent people—geniuses—blew their intellectual gifts and talents by not following the path of integrity of doing what's right.

LOSING THE WAY

The main lesson here—and in the cases of Bernie Madoff, Ivan Boesky, and others (and sadly, there are so many we can recount; sadder too is they are the only ones who make headlines, but there are many more on a smaller scale)—is that any of us can get too close, too driven, too robotic, and nonhuman. We can lose sight of our ethics (essential to our humanity)—or they can get murky. We need a team around us that keeps us on the straight and narrow, honest, and aligned with integrity to make sure that our vision is anchored to our core principles while still supporting visionary/out-of-the-box thinking. (Those around Holmes and Bankman-Fried did not do enough to challenge their reckless ways.) Thus, I am not suggesting to not dream big because that is what entrepreneurs and inventors do. "Go big or go home," as the saying goes. Change the world! Indeed, by all means. However, it can go too far without ethics, integrity, and compliance as part of the big picture. True leaders, exceptional leaders do not want to be surrounded by "yes-men" or "yes-women." Just ask Abraham Lincoln and his Civil War cabinet.

Incorporating the concept of ethics with compliance is critical. In other words it's about doing what's right, not just what's required. (Sorry, but I will repeat this often!) When I joined TAP Pharmaceuticals as their chief ethics and compliance and privacy officer, it was clear that the word "compliance" alone would not resonate with the company, which was principally a sales and marketing organization. *Compliance* does not shout "inspiration"—not even to me! Recognizing that, I needed to find a way to reach both hearts and minds to inspire compliance. That is when I realized if I wanted people to think about doing what is right, we needed to signal that by literally leading with the word "ethics." This is how I came to recommend to TAP Pharmaceuticals that instead of having a compliance program, they should have an *ethics and compliance* program. Fast-forward to today, and almost every life sciences company has an ethics and compliance program. Twenty-plus years ago, in late 2001, only TAP Pharmaceuticals had an ethics and compliance program. I am proud to have been part of the team that led the way!

Pharmaceutical companies are one of the largest advertisers in the world, pouring billions of dollars into television, radio, print, and social media advertising campaigns. Between 2011 and 2015, the pharmaceutical industry spent more than $20 billion in advertising dollars to promote drugs directly to consumers, nearly all of it on mass-market television.[12] In a single year, 2022, Big Pharma spent $8.1 billion on ads.[13] These strategies have influenced physicians' prescribing habits, increased drug utilization, and stimulated the demand for branded drugs. Consumer commercials are advocating going to our doctor to ask if a certain drug is right for us. However, very often, the list of side effects sounds worse than the actual medical condition. Plus, the actors in the commercial continue to smile as those side effects are rattled off with the sun shining in the background.

The pharmaceutical industry lost their way and got caught up in the competition of drugs without a moral anchor. They were swept up in the hurricane of competition. They engaged in an "entertainment arms race," seeing who could out-"wine and dine" doctors to get more scripts. They lost all sense of proportion, all sense of appropriate boundaries. As history has shown, sooner or later, the risk of not

---

12   John Singer, "The Problem That's Arrived for the Pharmaceutical Industry," Tincture, January 28, 2019, https://tincture.io/the-problem-thats-arrived-for-the-pharmaceutical-industry-8617e36adec4.

13   Ben Adams, "The Top 10 Pharma Drug Ad Spenders for 2022," fiercepharma.com, May 1, 2023, https://www.fiercepharma.com/special-reports/top-10-pharma-drug-brand-ad-spenders-2022.

having an effective ethics and compliance program, a system of checks and balances in place, will catch up with you.

Prevention Is Key

While you still want to be—indeed, in many ways, must be—that "discoverer," inventor, and innovator, you also must be smart about the path you walk. Compliance gets its negative reputation because, historically, it meant having risk-averse attorneys telling you no, no, and no. Today's modern compliance programs can be especially complex. You need a solution that integrates all the data, parts, and pieces to yield an in-depth understanding of your compliance program, indeed of your business risks. Without integration, your data can lack visibility, control, and measurable results. You need a system that surfaces trends in an intelligent manner and connects the dots between initiatives. That integration is key to prevention.

That prevention also needs to come from leadership. This includes leading with values and principles such as the following:

- Encouraging employee engagement

- Working together as a team

- Bringing in different perspectives to inform you as a leader

- Leading by example; living your ethics

- Remembering that leadership is about inspiring the people behind the product

Compliance is just one piece of a larger mosaic, but it's essential, especially in the life sciences industry, as people's lives and billions of dollars are at risk. Theranos did not have a chief ethics and compliance officer and only added one after the story broke, but it was too little, too late. FTX had a chief compliance officer named Dan Friedberg. Interestingly, he was, in 2008, tied to an online poker scandal involving $50 million in misappropriated funds.[14] Compliance is not a flavor of the month; it is not an afterthought. It must be integral to a company—to that company's profit and benefit.

You have to integrate ethics and compliance into your commercial and corporate DNA up front. Why? Because it takes time to develop trust, and trust is the essential ingredient for successful human relationships, including business relationships. You have to connect hearts and minds to be effective and to earn the trust of the people you are trying to lead. It has to be a culture of integrity and trust. And that has to start with *you* as the leader.

Theranos misrepresented the science behind the product, and the testing did not support the claims. Sam Bankman-Fried treated FTX as his personal ATM machine.

Ultimately, compliance is about business integrity.

Investors invest in the intelligence and energy of an entrepreneur to change the world; that is what investors buy. This is a key example of how a lack of moral leadership resulted in tragic outcomes. There were no checks and balances in place to catch the fraud.

In the life sciences, the industry landscape is riddled with corporate corpses—companies that paid the reputational and financial penalties associated with government indictments and settlement agreements.

Here is a list of some of the top twenty pharmaceutical settlements in the United States, starting with the TAP case in 2001:

---

14   Daniel Kuhn, Xinyu Luo, and David Morris, "Who's Who in the FTX Inner Circle," coindesk.com, November 27, 2022, https://www.coindesk.com/layer2/2022/11/22/the-whos-who-of-the-ftx-inner-circle/.

1. **TAP Pharmaceuticals**—$875 million (2001): Settlement related to fraudulent pricing and marketing practices for the drug Lupron.

2. **Sanofi-Aventis**—$109 million (2007): Settlement for alleged drug pricing fraud.

3. **Valeant Pharmaceuticals** (formerly Biovail)—$95 million (2008): Settlement for accounting fraud and misreporting earnings.

4. **Pfizer**—$2.3 billion (2009): Settlement for illegal marketing practices, including off-label promotion, involving drugs such as Bextra and Lyrica.

5. **Eli Lilly**—$1.4 billion (2009): Settlement for off-label promotion of the antipsychotic drug Zyprexa.

6. **Forest Laboratories**—$313 million (2010): Settlement for off-label marketing and kickbacks related to several drugs.

7. **Novartis**—$678 million (2010): Settlement for off-label marketing of several drugs, including Trileptal and Diovan.

8. **AstraZeneca**—$520 million (2010): Settlement for off-label marketing of the antipsychotic drug Seroquel.

9. **Merck & Co.**—$950 million (2011): Settlement for marketing Vioxx for unapproved uses and concealing cardiovascular risks.

10. **GlaxoSmithKline**—$3 billion (2012): Settlement for healthcare fraud allegations, including unlawful promotion of prescription drugs and failure to report safety data.

11. **Abbott Laboratories**—$1.6 billion (2012): Settlement for allegations of off-label marketing of the antiepileptic drug Depakote.

12. **Amgen**—$762 million (2012): Settlement for allegations of improper marketing practices related to several drugs, including Aranesp.

13. **Boehringer Ingelheim**—$650 million (2012): Settlement for manufacturing issues with certain drugs and off-label marketing of the stroke-prevention drug Pradaxa.

14. **Johnson & Johnson**—$2.2 billion (2013): Settlement related to the marketing of Risperdal, an antipsychotic medication, and other drugs.

15. **GlaxoSmithKline**—$105 million (2016): Settlement for manufacturing issues at a plant in Puerto Rico and allegations of product quality.

16. **Mylan**—$465 million (2016): Settlement for underpaying Medicaid rebates for the EpiPen.

17. **Teva Pharmaceutical Industries**—$519 million (2016): Settlement for paying kickbacks to promote its generic drugs.

18. **Endo Health Solutions**—$192.7 million (2017): Settlement related to the marketing of the prescription drug Lidoderm for unapproved uses.

19. **Celgene Corporation**—$280 million (2017): Settlement for promoting two cancer drugs for unapproved uses.

20. **Purdue Pharma (OxyContin)**—$8.3 billion (2020): Settlement for its role in the opioid epidemic.

But it doesn't have to be this way for you. You can challenge the status quo and still prevent this corporate carnage from happening to you with the right leadership and governance. Plugging in ethics and compliance at the beginning is key as you steer your company to success, avoiding all the rocks and shoals that can sink you. If you are an up-and-coming lawyer or someone interested in going into compliance, you will be integral to preventing this nightmare from happening to your clients.

But keep in mind, better late than never. So if you have not initiated an ethics and compliance program, do not delay any longer.

Balance Government Regulation with Free Enterprise and Leadership

The goal of regulations is to enhance, not undermine, the well-being of society. Regulations should do more good than harm. Unfortunately, that has not always been the case. In my opinion, and the opinion of many others, we have had too much regulation that adds unnecessary costs and little value. Nevertheless, our government certainly has an appropriate role and responsibility to ensure the safety and efficacy of pharmaceutical products, as well as a fiscal responsibility to protect taxpayer dollars from fraud and abuse. Make no mistake, there has been considerable fraud and abuse in the pharmaceutical industry. There have also been several tragic examples of drugs that caused a great deal of harm—such as the thalidomide tragedy in the 1960s, DES in the 1970s, and more recent scandals such as Vioxx, Bextra, Rezulin, and Seldane.[15]

Today's modern leader needs to appreciate the need for a collaborative public/private partnership that combines appropriate government regulation with free enterprise to publicly promote drugs, which was illegal up until 1983.

---

15   Douglas A. McIntyre, "The Ten Worst Drug Recalls in the History of the FDA," 247wallst.com, December 10, 2010, https://247wallst.com/investing/2010/12/10/the-ten-worst-drug-recalls-in-the-history-of-the-fda/.

A good example of such a modern leader, whom I had the pleasure to work with, was Mr. Miles White, who served as CEO of Abbott Laboratories. He retired in 2020. Abbott specializes in cardiovascular, diagnostics, diabetes, and neuromodulation products. Abbott is also well known for its pediatric and adult nutrition brands including Pedialyte, Ensure, Glucerna, and Similac.

By most objective standards, Miles White was a very successful CEO and a real visionary. Back in the early 2000s, when I was working as the TAP VP, chief ethics and compliance officer, it came to my attention that Miles was going to be named the industry representative CEO of the Pharmaceutical Research and Manufacturers of America (PhRMA). (TAP was a joint venture between Abbott and Takeda.) At the time Abbott Labs was also putting their own compliance program in place, and I requested a meeting with Miles to talk about the opportunity he had as the incoming PhRMA CEO. Much to my nervous excitement, he agreed to see me.

Hearing that he was quite the history buff, I brought a PBS tape of Theodore Roosevelt, who founded the FDA and was considered a progressive for his time nearly a hundred years earlier.

I said to Miles, "This is a great opportunity for you to represent the industry and make some meaningful change to restore consumer confidence in the industry, in the spirit of Teddy Roosevelt when he created the FDA to protect the public from snake oil salesmen."

"Our reputation is mud." Miles shook his head. "We have to do something."

"Yes, this is your opportunity to do something good," I responded. "At the end of the day, it is about the patients."

At the time, ironically, this was not the case. The pharmaceutical industry was focused on doctors, the script writers. Fast-forward twenty or so years to today, and every company is focused on patients.

Why? Direct-to-consumer commercials took off on television in the early 1990s, creating a huge change, a huge disruption (and billions of ad spend, as we just discussed). Increasingly, the individual consumer now has the power to influence their doctor. With some very equivalent products on the market, all else being equal, typically, the doctor is going to give the patient what they want. A patient can say, "I want this drug," and the doctor can make the decision to prescribe the requested drug, with a key caveat—subject to insurance and what it will or will not cover.

Insurance seeks to limit costs. As a result generics are preferred by insurance over name-brand drugs. Why? Money. They are cheaper. You might get a letter in the mail stating something to the effect, "We can make your drug costs go down if you use a generic form." While on the one hand, patients may have more opportunities to influence their healthcare decisions, many, especially the elderly, may still feel relatively powerless.

Doctors who are focused on rare diseases prescribe therapies that often require significant product and patient support; often, nurse educators will then educate patients in the proper care and use of the product. Many of these products are injectables. Done improperly, however, this support has the potential to appear and to be, in fact, a kickback.

In the "Wild West" nineties, companies engaged in an "entertainment arms race"—it was all about who could beat the other company in entertaining doctors—dinners, junkets in vacation hot spots, etc. This all came crashing to earth in the early 2000s as the government cracked down on these practices as violations of the federal Anti-Kickback and False Claims Acts. What ensued over several years was a series of megasettlements of hundreds of millions of dollars and ultimately reaching into the multiple billions of dollars, as shown in the table earlier in the chapter.

Today, rare disease biotech companies, which deal with life-and-death diseases, cater to a very small population of patients, interact with a very small circle of world-renowned experts, and promote extraordinarily expensive drugs that require extensive education and support. As a result, rather than out-entertain each other with doctors, companies are trying to out-support each other and market their services to patients. It's the same commercially driven competitive landscape, manifesting equally risky compliance behavior but with a different twist and focus.

What remains today is a highly competitive environment for companies trying to win market share with salespeople who have aggressive sales goals that push the envelope. This is where an effective ethics and compliance program can act as a check-and-balance protocol that shows when and where you might cross the line and when you need to pull back. One final point: even the most senior board members and executives continue to check out competitors to see if they are doing the same thing, as I am often asked, "What are other companies doing?"

A look at the history of compliance enforcement shows that following what other companies are doing is often a road to disaster. In the early 2000s, what used to be standard industry practice in the 1990s became illegal criminal activity almost overnight. The companies caught in the web of sudden enforcement include some of the largest pharmaceutical companies in the world, to include Pfizer, Abbott, Bayer, AstraZeneca, Johnson & Johnson, Eli Lilly, and GlaxoSmithKline (GSK), as shown in the earlier table. Each of these companies had (and continues to have) veritable legions of lawyers and compliance professionals advising them and working on their behalf, yet each suffered massive financial and reputational losses and entered into federal settlements.

How could this happen? To understand this outcome, it is important to step back and understand the broader historical and business context of the time. As stated earlier what was legal (or thought to be) in the 1990s became illegal in the early 2000s. That pattern continues today. Companies should not gauge what is right or wrong by common industry practice or what others are doing. Rather, companies should be guided by core principles and values. They should always test any strategy or any proposed activity against these core values, which fundamentally focus on two things: (1) safety and (2) efficacy.

Getting back to Miles White's (Abbott) story, he appreciated the historical reference and asked for a copy of the video. In fact, at a separate conference, he proudly acknowledged our efforts at TAP to implement effective and meaningful change in our ethics and compliance program.

Today, if you walk down the corridor of any biotech company, you will likely see signs and pictures of patients with slogans such as "We put patients first." Why?

1. Patients are more actively involved in requesting their own scripts and can influence the impact of prescriptions that have direct financial results.

2. The nature of the products, whether they are specialty pharma or orphan drugs—drugs that are not developed by the pharmaceutical industry for economic reasons but which respond to public health need—often requires the science of individualized therapies based on genetics with RNA and DNA or scientific discoveries.

3. Applying these therapies can include injectables and require more communication with the patient.

4. This positioning is socially and politically more acceptable, legally more defensible, and it results in more sales.

So how do you strike the right balance in this high-risk, high-reward environment and win with compliance? You inspire integrity! You must never forget that at its core, any ethics and compliance program is about affecting *the behavior* of people to achieve specific outcomes. To do so, you must connect with their hearts and minds and inspire and motivate them to comply, to have them *want to comply*! As a leader, when you connect to the mind, you are appealing to the logical, data-driven, evidence-seeking, rational side of a person. When you connect to the heart, you are appealing to the passionate, emotional side, to core values that generate pride and trust. You must integrate your message of ethics and compliance, one that fuses the rational with the emotional, that unites hearts with minds, and that instills the trust and understanding that will yield acceptance, support, and success.

As a retired Florida congressman once said to me, "What people forget is that it is not enough to simply persuade. You have to *motivate* people to turn out and vote and pull the lever." Developing that motivation, that inspiration to enable the vision and mission of the company—to bring lifesaving/life-improving therapies to patients and their families—is the reason people will want to comply.

In the next chapter, we are going to focus on how to create a culture of ethics and integrity.

CHAPTER 2:

CREATING A CULTURE OF ETHICS AND INTEGRITY: LEADERSHIP IN ACTION

Creating a culture of integrity and accountability not only improves effectiveness, but it also generates a respectful, enjoyable, and life-giving setting in which to work.

—BYRON R. PULSIFER

As a Marine I had a close-up view of leadership in action. I understood, as I shared in chapter 1, that the tone at the top sets the tone for the rest of the organization; therefore, a leader determines how ethics and compliance is perceived—whether embraced or not. However, even a positive, enthusiastic, inspirational leader who motivates people to embrace compliance is, by itself, not enough. Leaders continue to be held responsible for poor conduct and poor performance, and companies are being pushed by customers, employees, and the government to step up and adopt a multistakeholder approach that serves both investor demands and the purpose of the company.

As a Marine, I understood that leadership, ethics, purpose, and character were essential. As the son of a doctor, I understood that technical skill combined with ethics and integrity needed to be woven into my very being. Anything less was unacceptable. So a "checking a box approach"—such as asking your employees to fill out a form that checks all the boxes to certify they have read all required materials or completed a compliance training course to comply with the law—is not enough. Leaders, especially in the life sciences industry, need to do more. There are some specific tactical steps that the organization needs to take to establish a foundation of ethics and integrity.

Develop a Mission Statement

When you commit to the Marines, you are making a *lifetime* commitment. It is a commitment to the very best ideals and traditions of the Marine Corps—selfless service, honor, integrity, discipline, strength, reliability, dependability, and a dedication to defending the US Constitution and the freedoms it represents. You may leave the service when your tour or commitment is up, but you will always be a Marine. "Once a Marine, always a Marine!" Every Marine knows that it's all about mission accomplishment.

Congressman Bill Clinger (R-PA), then Chairman of the House Government Operations Committee, US House of Representatives, congratulating me on my promotion to Major, circa 1994

In the corporate world, a mission statement should also feel binding and important to your company and your people. It is also incredibly important that they view it as a part of who they are, of why they get up and go to work every day for the company.

Put another way, you need to set a North Star. Your corporate star should be a guide built on principles and values that frame the direction for your company. If you are a founder or CEO, you have a wonderful opportunity to do that. In fact, one thing I think is exciting is that a compliance program can be a great vehicle to weave those principles into the concept of

Doing what's right, not just what's required.

Being legally compliant should be a subset of being ethical. You can't accomplish the mission without being both ethical and legally compliant, particularly in the world of healthcare, where every action may affect people's lives and well-being.

Healthcare, as we will emphasize throughout this book, is very different from any other business. You have to have genuine empathy for people, for patients who will use your products and services. Everyone has to be bought into that from the top down, from the bottom up. Everyone has to know that it is the company's mission, the company's North Star. Everyone should be inspired and motivated as to why this company exists and the direction in which it's going because that will unleash the passion, the energy, the inspiration, the excitement that you need every day to excel, to be the best.

I like to use the example that as a Marine, no matter your military occupational specialty, everyone shares in the commitment to the core mission of the Marines, which is led by the infantry. For example, I was an artillery officer, then a lawyer, and then an intelligence officer. Nevertheless, I was trained as all Marines are that the mission of the infantry is the core mission of the Marine Corps. All Marines are trained as to what the infantry is all about and then how we fit into that broader mosaic to support the infantry mission to achieve mission accomplishment as a team.

You can see that same concept in the life sciences. Again, it is all about helping to create therapies or even cures to improve people's lives with medication, with medical devices. That is the core mission; that is the point, the raison d'être for the company. Every person in the company has to buy into that mission. That's the point of a mission statement and a values statement.

Build consensus with the executive team as to what the core values and mission of the company are by developing a mission statement that represents the culture and identity of what the company stands for. Of course, this must be led by the senior leader, CEO, or president of the company.

A successful mission statement should be as follows:

- Simple. A mission statement is no good if people can't remember it.

- Inspirational. No one works passionately … to be mediocre. A mission statement should offer people a bold vision.

- Unique. What are *your* company and *your* values? Your mission statement should reflect that.

Here is an example of a mission statement we created for the TAP Pharmaceuticals Compliance Team:

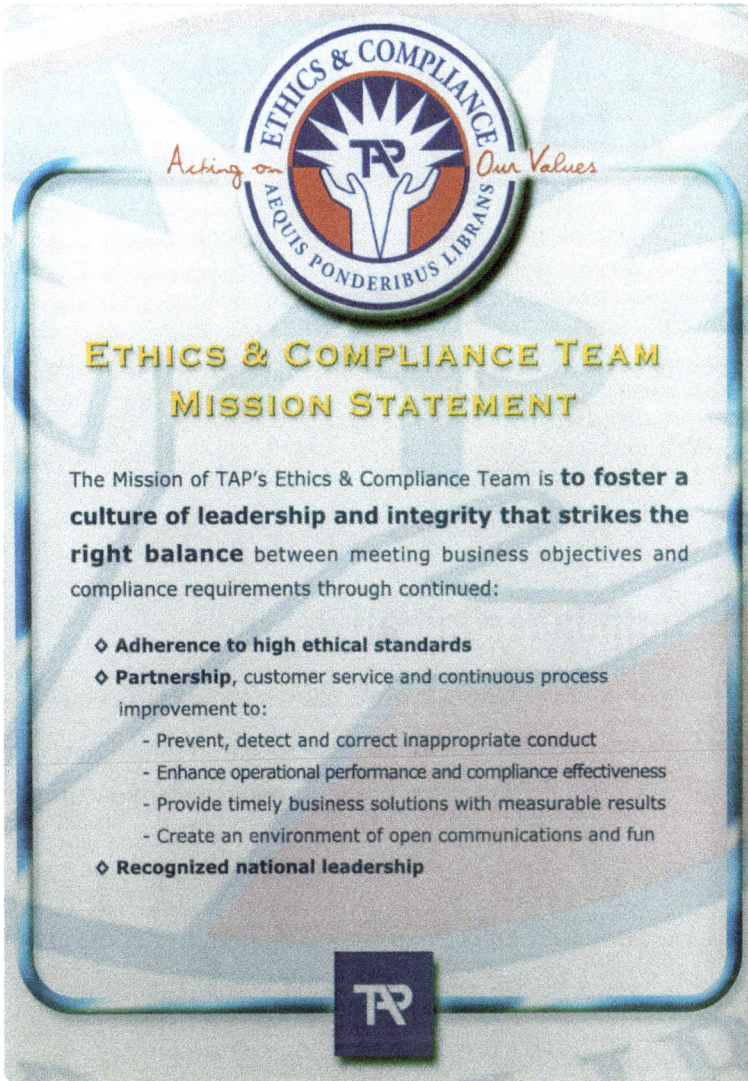

ETHICS & COMPLIANCE TEAM
MISSION STATEMENT

The Mission of TAP's Ethics & Compliance Team is **to foster a culture of leadership and integrity that strikes the right balance** between meeting business objectives and compliance requirements through continued:

◇ **Adherence to high ethical standards**
◇ **Partnership**, customer service and continuous process improvement to:
  - Prevent, detect and correct inappropriate conduct
  - Enhance operational performance and compliance effectiveness
  - Provide timely business solutions with measurable results
  - Create an environment of open communications and fun
◇ **Recognized national leadership**

The Mission of TAP's Ethics and Compliance Team is to foster a culture of leadership and integrity that strikes the right balance between meeting business objectives and compliance requirements through continued:

- *Adherence to high ethical standards*
- *Partnership, customer service, and continuous process improvement to:*

- □ *Prevent, detect, and correct inappropriate conduct*
- □ *Enhance operational performance and compliance effectiveness*
- □ *Provide timely business solutions with measurable results*
- □ *Create an environment of open communication and fun*

- *Recognized national leadership*

Notice how this list quite literally *leads* with ethics (something I mentioned earlier in the book). Yet there are other mission-critical elements that all employees should embrace—right down to creating an environment of fun.

The Compliance Initiative

Even if you do not yet have a compliance officer in place, you can use the compliance initiative as a platform to create a values-driven, principles-driven organization. One of the biggest challenges companies and compliance officers face is implementing a new compliance initiative. In many cases these initiatives can often be a response to something that occurred or went wrong (which is one reason why I wrote this book—to convince you to have compliance as part of the lifeblood of your company from its very origins). The truth is that most compliance initiatives are the result of responses to identified compliance problems and violations and/or changing laws and regulations (and trust me, they are always changing!).

My consulting company, TRESTLE Compliance, often deals with smaller-cap life sciences companies that are about to make the pivot from a research and development–based company to a commercial one. They are either preparing to launch their very first product they have submitted to the FDA for approval, or they have one product and are looking to build out their portfolio and develop other products. Thus, they often need an added boost of expertise and support (i.e., to add more "firepower" to their compliance program). We also consult with companies that are outside of the United States (e.g., the United Kingdom or Canada) that are looking to launch in the United States as their primary market. They're developing and recruiting a US sales force and need a US commercial compliance expert who is familiar with developing and implementing an effective compliance program. All of these companies usually do not have the in-house expertise, particularly if they are a start-up company. The CEO is generally an MD, PhD scientist, and the corporate lawyer, if they have one, is focused on intellectual property and corporate law.

Commercialization and the nuances of selling FDA-approved products and the associated risks and enforcement focus in this area mean effective commercial compliance is a necessity. I am often contacted and "dropped into the hot zone" after something has already gone wrong, when a company needs to "reset" or when they're in a crisis mode and need a compliance expert to come in to calmly develop and execute an effective compliance approach to help avert or mitigate a crisis, often working with outside and in-house counsels and operational business leaders.

THE WARNER CHILCOTT CASE

The scenario I just described is exactly what happened at Warner Chilcott. I had just one hundred days to completely redesign and rebuild a compliance program, assemble a compliance team, develop, roll out, and more—*but* it doesn't have to be that dramatic. It shouldn't require a compliance emergency response. You just need to get it right up front.

We turned the existing company logo consisting of the letters WC into a tagline of "Winning with Compliance." This goes along with the idea I just shared that it must be memorable. Winning with Compliance is easy to recall—and says a great deal.

This is just another reminder to make compliance part of your DNA from the beginning!

Connect with Something You Believe In

Increasingly, people want to work for companies whose values reflect their own. One survey noted that 54 percent of respondents would take a pay cut in order to work for a company that shares their values,[16] while 40 percent said they would *quit* their job if their company took a political position they did not agree with.[17]

People will embrace compliance if it is predicated on something they can embrace and believe in. This is where words matter. Develop a mission statement and build a compliance program around that mission. Simon Sinek once tweeted, "Customers will never love a company until the employees love it first."[18]

I might adjust that a little: customers will not believe in your company and your mission until your employees believe in it first. In fact, your customers will not trust your company until your employees trust it first.

---

16   Stephanie Dhue and Sharon Epperson, "Most Workers Want Their Employer to Share Their Values," updated July 6, 2022, https://www.cnbc.com/2022/07/01/most-workers-want-their-employer-to-share-their-values.html.

17   Ibid.

18   Matthew Toren, "How These 8 Founders Are Innovating Company Culture," Entrepreneur.com, June 30, 2016, https://www.entrepreneur.com/growing-a-business/how-these-8-founders-are-innovating-company-culture/278358.

You have to be clear about what the compliance program is all about and be consistent. It is not just a legal checklist of policies and procedures—that will inspire no one.

HIGHER PURPOSE

How do you make a compliance program real? You have to equate it to a higher purpose. So for example, your company's higher purpose might be to eradicate juvenile diabetes. However, the bigger picture is not returns on dividends but saving and improving the lives of real-life patients while also returning shareholder value. You need to integrate values, principles, and integrity into compliance while recognizing the fiduciary responsibility of returning value to investors. The two go together. You want to create a credible culture of compliance, a culture of integrity, one in which people are vested and believe. The key word is *credible*. That takes hard work that goes beyond just appealing to the rational mind of your audience. You need to inspire them. You need to inspire their integrity to achieve compliance.

COMPLYING WITH THE MISSION

Once you have a values and mission statement, you then have to ensure that the different elements of the compliance program reflect those values. The compliance program's core component elements allow you to operate consistently, across all departments, as an integrated whole. Communicated correctly, it will resonate within the company with purpose and meaning, always answering the questions, "Why do we need to comply?" and "Why should we want to comply?" With continuous effective communications by leadership about the higher purpose and mission of the company and the importance of compliance in meeting that purpose and mission, you will keep compliance front of mind and indeed inspiring integrity and reap the benefits of a *culture of compliance.*

THE BIG PICTURE

As leaders are consumed with other priorities, it may be tempting to think of a compliance program as nothing but a bunch of rules and regulations driven by legal requirements from your legal team. As I have been emphasizing throughout this book, think of compliance as something that is tied to something larger (e.g., to the healthcare mission to cure a disease or improve the lives of patients). If you are new to compliance, you must know that your mission is to support not only that vision but also that leader and CEO, that visionary, in such a way that they can bring their vision, their cure, their treatment to fruition in an ethical way.

To illustrate, let me reshare a well-known story about John F. Kennedy visiting NASA in 1962 as our country was embarking on the mission of landing a man on the moon. Kennedy noticed a janitor standing off to the side with a broom. He walked over and introduced himself and said, "I'm Jack Kennedy. What do you do?" The janitor replied, "I'm helping to put a man on the moon."[19]

This story illustrates that every person in your organization is part of the bigger mission, the bigger picture. They should each take pride of ownership in what it is you are trying to do. It is like every Marine, regardless of rank, being part of the corpus that unites us all in one purpose. Positioning compliance as supporting that big picture, that core mission will position it as a credible supporting component that will be more readily accepted and, as a result, be more effective. It will succeed to inspire and motivate people to want to support that

---

19   John Nemo, "What a NASA Janitor Can Teach Us about Living a Bigger Life," Bizjournals. com, December 23, 2014, https://www.bizjournals.com/bizjournals/how-to/growth-strate-gies/2014/12/what-a-nasa-janitor-can-teach-us.html.

mission, to want to do what's right for that mission, to indeed want to comply with whatever it takes to accomplish that mission.

LEAD BY EXAMPLE

The other key aspect of ethics and integrity is leadership by example, something we will continue to come back to. You can create a program of values and principles, but if you don't act on those as the CEO, president, or board member, then all of this will be worthless. Leaders can dish out what they want the company to represent, but what are your core values?

I am sure we have all known someone who embodied the concept of "do as I say, not as I do." That mindset can be incredibly discouraging and disheartening to the people around them.

Instead, create a handful of core values that can be easily remembered.

Values can include key words such as the following:

- Integrity

- Respect

- Excellence

- Transparency

- Trust

- Ingenuity

- Honesty

Follow up those values with actions that match, help your employees and staff understand why the procedures are necessary, make them easily accessible, and reward employees who comply with and embrace the program.

Meet Those Values

A compliance program without ethics and integrity, historically, has been seen as a lawyer-driven program, a dry, boring compilation of irritating and annoying checklists for the purpose of legally defending the company if it gets into trouble. It's often perceived as a necessary evil driven by lawyers for lawyers to provide CYA for a company that everyone else has to suffer through and be burdened with. That, unfortunately, is not only the perception but also the reality with companies that rely on a pure legal approach to compliance. Yet it is the approach that most executives and employees alike both fear and loathe—for good reasons.

As we have emphasized, it need not be that way. Integrating core components of ethics and values that emphasize integrity applied for the purpose of achieving the purpose, the mission of the company will give meaning, depth, and credibility to the compliance program. Living by a credible moral compass gets people to sit up and pay attention. Feeling proud to be associated with a company that runs its business by doing what is right, not just what is required, is the formula for creating a culture of compliance, a culture of ethics and integrity.

Compliance is about building a reputation for being the best you can be and taking pride in that reputation. When you are passionate about quality and growth with compliance, then people will embrace that opportunity to grow and be the best in your specialty or industry.

Each person in the company, starting at the top with the CEO, president, and board members, is a vital link in the chain and recognizes their importance in the bigger picture and mission. Pride comes with a realization that you are making a difference in this world. Creating a culture of ethics and integrity that shows what you stand for—this is how you win with compliance.

In the next chapter, we will address the importance of structure in an effective compliance program.

CHAPTER 3:

A FRAMEWORK FOR SUCCESS: THE IMPORTANCE OF STRUCTURE

Grasping the structure of a subject is understanding it in a way that permits many other things to be related to it meaningfully. To learn structure in short, is to learn how things are related.

—JEROME S. BRUNER

istorically, the evolution of compliance starts with a reaction to a problem. Sometimes, there is a compliance response team; often, a CEO wisely seeks the advice of outside counsel, who, in turn, often brings in compliance experts. Companies often react to the compliance problems of another company to prevent the same problems in their company. Unfortunately, these reactions are often quick, knee-jerk reactions that are often isolated and limited to addressing a specific issue. They are reactive, not proactive. Companies that respond in this way often do not have a compliance program in place. Rather than spending the time and money to establish a broader, holistic compliance framework, many companies, especially smaller companies, are tempted to address compliance issues in this piecemeal fashion. Why? They fall prey to the temptation of a flawed cost/benefit analysis that tends to underestimate compliance risks and overestimate the relative cost of taking a more holistic, more effective comprehensive approach. This is understandable if you are trying to start a new company and/or launch a new product where every dollar counts and time is of the essence. But while expensive law firms and Big Four accounting firms can indeed be cost prohibitive (I know—I used to work at a Big Four firm, where we sold the brand at premium prices), there are now other more affordable and equally, or even more, effective options.

While you may think establishing a compliance program is costly, what is *truly* costly is a class action lawsuit, a massive setback in bringing a product to market, and dealing with the reputational fallout of such a scandal. Beyond that, as the mother in the video I talked about early in the book made clear, the true costs of a failure of compliance are the devasting impact it has on the lives of patients and their families who are depending on your company to survive and produce new therapies that may save or improve their lives.

From a compliance effectiveness perspective, putting in a comprehensive compliance framework is a bit like getting a vaccine—you do it to prevent and avoid a much more serious outcome. Believing that it is cheaper to address compliance problems issue by issue is a bit like playing *Whack-A-Mole*—you will always be reacting and never know where the next problem will occur. Over time, this can consume significant time, effort, and expense.

The far better, more effective, and credible solution is to put in place a properly scaled, risk-based preventive compliance framework.

When it comes to implementing a compliance program, it may seem like climbing Mount Everest. Where do you begin? Well, as with any undertaking entailing significant risks, you bring on an experienced expert to help you get to the top … and back again! So think of a compliance consultant as a sherpa. The investment in the right sherpa will ensure not just survival and avoiding costly and even lethal mistakes but also success in meeting the challenge and doing it well. The bottom line is that retaining the right expert to guide you and to build the right holistic compliance structure is incredibly important to having an effective compliance program.

A Brief History of Compliance in Healthcare

Those who don't know history are doomed to repeat it.

—EDMUND BURKE

Back in the late 1980s, something called the US Sentencing Commission was created. It was originally intended to address divergent sentences in different federal courts, particularly in the area of drug enforcement. For example, if you were in California, you might get a much lighter sentence for a crime than in Texas. There was a consensus that this issue needed to be addressed and rectified in the spirit of justice for all in the federal justice system.

The Sentencing Commission created sentencing guidelines for federal judges to apply when evaluating and determining the appropriate sentence for someone convicted of a federal crime. This applied to corporate entities, as well as individuals. It was in the context of corporate convictions that the Sentencing Commission developed the concept of a compliance program and the key elements that could provide some mitigating value to companies during sentencing.

Fast-forward to the mid-1990s, when the Office of Inspector General from the Department of Health and Human Services (OIG-

DHHS) decided to write compliance guidances for various sectors of the healthcare industry.

After the 1992 presidential election, President Clinton had his wife, attorney Hillary Clinton, lead a healthcare task force to recommend reform initiatives. The process was criticized for a lack of transparency, and the then Republican Congress failed to approve any of the healthcare reforms recommended by the task force. (I happened to be serving as a Republican professional staff member [defense counsel] working on national security issues for the National Security Subcommittee on the House Government Reform and Oversight Committee from 1992 to 1995.)

The professional staff of the House Government Reform and Oversight Committee with Chairman Bill Clinger (R-PA), 1993 (that's me standing with the striped tie, second to the last on the right)

However, after these healthcare initiatives were rejected, President Clinton's Department of Justice (DOJ) declared war on healthcare fraud, with healthcare cited as the DOJ's number two enforcement priority after organized crime. That's not a coincidence. A few years later, in the late 1990s, former attorney general Dick Thornburgh took me aside when we were both speakers at a conference in Washington. He said, "Steve, one thing people should always understand, when the Department of Justice declares war on something as a number one, two, or three top priority, guaranteed, two things will happen. There will be more indictments and more convictions."

It is in that context that the healthcare industry changed in the 1990s. Mergers and acquisitions became extremely common. National networks of privately owned and managed hospitals were built, with Columbia HCA being the most notable, with the concept of creating greater efficiency and value based on the *business* bottom line. The medical billing industry under this new model was rife with potential illegal activities relative to Medicare and Medicaid, which led to greater federal scrutiny for healthcare fraud.

As the very first compliance officer recruited to the largest and only publicly traded medical billing company, Medaphis, which had just come under federal investigation, I was very involved in developing the compliance standards for that industry. Leveraging my preexisting positive relationships with members of the OIG Legal Counsel's Office, I helped write the OIG guidance for the medical billing industry, submitting the first draft as a paid consultant working on behalf of the industry association, the International Billing and Management Association, now renamed and known as the Healthcare Billing and Management Association (HBMA). Fast-forward to the early 2000s. The pharmaceutical industry by this time came within the crosshairs of the DOJ and the OIG. Why? The government was following the money. Healthcare (and national defense) is where the most federal healthcare dollars are spent, through federal programs such as Medicare, Medicaid, and TRICARE. As the 2000s progressed, big-name companies began falling like dominoes with huge multi-million-dollar settlements that eventually grew to multibillion-dollar settlements with the DOJ and OIG, as shown in our earlier table.

In telling this story, I must confess I feel a bit like the Forrest Gump of compliance (but only if Forrest Gump had been a Marine!). Why? Well, beyond the Washington, DC, and military connections, I did find myself in the thick of things with the medical billing industry's compliance evolution and, soon thereafter, at the center of the pharmaceutical industry's compliance "hot zone." Specifically, I was recruited to serve as the first chief compliance and privacy officer for TAP Pharmaceuticals in September 2001—right before 9/11 (and right before my birthday, as it so happened). Happy birthday, Steve! Welcome to TAP! Wow! Talk about drinking from a fire hose! At $885 million, this was at the time the first major and largest settlement in the history of the pharmaceutical industry. It addressed inappropriate sales and marketing practices stretching back to 1995. The corporate integrity agreement (CIA) agreed to by TAP with the OIG was the first of its kind. No one had ever tackled this before. Being new to the company, not to mention without any prior pharmaceutical industry experience, combined with strict federal deadlines all compounded by the shock of 9/11 and the shock of the settlement on the company, put a bright, sharp spotlight on this critical and enormous Mt. Everest–type of mission that this Marine had accepted as his latest challenge. Applying my training from my parents, from my education, from the Marines, from my time serving in the cutthroat trenches in the halls of Congress as a professional staff member, and from cutting my teeth in the compliance world in the medical billing industry, I successfully built a team, developed a plan, and executed the mission successfully. Clearly, I am living proof that the most important ingredient to building and leading an effective compliance program is not industry-specific experience. Of course, it certainly helps, and in fairness, timing is everything. No one at that time had that kind of experience. But it goes to my overall point that effective compliance is more about effective leadership than about specific technical requirements, which can be learned more readily. Leadership, like trust, takes time to cultivate.

Speaking of time, I know this may sound strange today, but back in the late 1990s and early 2000s, the concept of risk as a legal matter, and more specifically, the word "risk" itself, was actually forbidden by some GCs of companies, including the one I worked with at TAP. Our GC said, "We can't even talk about risks. It's forbidden. Don't even write that word down because it may be prima facie evidence that we accept anything less than zero tolerance when it comes to compliance."

In fairness, he had a point at the time. I had attended a conference in Washington, DC, in the late 1990s where a senior counsel for the Department of the Treasury speaking as part of a federal agency panel openly declared that any compliance failure for any company would be considered prima facia evidence of the ineffectiveness of the compliance program. Myself and, as it turns out, two members of the OIG legal team who happened to be seated next to me were aghast at what we had each heard. We looked at each other and asked, "So perfection is the standard? That can't be right." And guess what, it's not. Fortunately, now twenty-five or so years later, there has been a complete 180-degree change on how "risk" is perceived relative to compliance program effectiveness. In fact, the DOJ, in its most recent compliance program evaluation guidance titled "U.S. Department of Justice Criminal Division Evaluation of Corporate Compliance Programs" stresses the importance of risk assessments. (I will review this guidance in greater detail later in the book.)

Similarly, you can see all over the OIG website the concept of risk: that you really need to weigh your risk, balance your risk, and ensure that you're prioritizing your risks.

The main point here is that, similar to any undertaking, before you go through it, you need to have taken an honest, credible assessment. Just like at a health club where you get an evaluation before you start your fitness program, you asses your strengths and weaknesses.

What Is Structure When It Comes to Compliance?

The structure of compliance is an overarching framework that is built into the design of the program with key components that include a governance process that ensures regular, credible oversight by the board and senior executive team. It is much like building a house where you need a blueprint to follow to establish a solid foundation from which to complete the home. A complete compliance program should be carefully designed and scaled to the risks of the company it is intended to support.

So first, conduct a thoughtful risk assessment, and then design an implementation plan that is carefully tailored to the specific risks of the business. This should not take longer than ninety days for smaller to midsize companies.

Second, don't make the classic mistake of either over- or under-estimating your risks by doing it yourself. The late great Nobel Prize laureate and Princeton economist Dr. Daniel Kahneman wrote eloquently and extensively about decision-making tendencies of under- and overestimation of risk and how to guard against it in his book *Thinking, Fast and Slow*. I had the honor and privilege of meeting Dr. Kahneman in the late 1990s as a student at the Harvard Executive Education course on Effective Decision-Making. You need an *independent*, experienced professional, a "compliance sherpa," for maximum credibility and maximum effectiveness. There is just too much at risk if you get it wrong.

When it comes to structure, creating a governance process is critically important, specifically by creating a charter for the compliance program. The charter must be reviewed and approved by the board of directors, together with a code of conduct or code of business ethics, which is also board reviewed and approved. Why is this important? You want this code of conduct to be part of the board DNA; it is tangible evidence of active board oversight of the compliance program, where the board has taken action to ensure appropriate internal controls are in place.

GOVERNANCE WITH A CHARTER

To understand this aspect of corporate governance, we need to go back to the 1996 In re: Caremark decision by the Delaware Court of Chancery.[20]

In the groundbreaking *Caremark* decision, the Delaware Court of Chancery set forth conditions for a corporate director's breach of their "fiduciary duty of loyalty" for oversight failures. These failures may occur if "(a) directors utterly failed to implement any reporting or information system or controls; or (b) having implemented such a system or controls, consciously failed to monitor or oversee its

---

20   *IN RE CAREMARK INTERN. INC. DERIV. LIT*, 698 A.2d 959 (Del. Ch. 1996), https://casetext.com/case/in-re-caremark-intern-inc-deriv-lit.

operations thus disabling themselves from being informed of risks or problems requiring their attention."

With that decision the court made clear that part of a director's fiduciary duty includes implementing and overseeing a company's compliance program.

Prior to that seminal decision, boards felt safe from prosecution because of the business judgment rule, which gave great deference to any action the board was doing, because it was premised on the concept that boards are acting in good faith for the benefit of the company. Thus, prior to *Caremark*, companies had to effectively demonstrate that the board was not acting in good faith—a high bar of proof. But what's different in the *Caremark* case is that the board took no action. It was in the face of complete inaction that the court said, in effect, "You [the board] did nothing. But you have a fiduciary duty to oversee the company, particularly the audit committee. That is your job. You took zero action, so therefore you're liable."

I have cited this case for years as to why board members need to be briefed regularly by the compliance officer, why they need to be kept informed about the specifics, why they need to be trained. The charter and the code of conduct all are sent up to the board for their review and approval, which is evidence of their active oversight. So incorporating the board into an active role of the compliance program is essential. Compliance must be part of the board's DNA too.

COMPLIANCE COMMITTEE

When it comes to governance, a company needs to establish an executive-level compliance committee where the key functional areas of the company are represented. The purpose of the compliance committee is twofold:

1. To ensure the compliance officer, who chairs the committee, receives input from the committee, who represents key functional areas of the company, to ensure the compliance program is responsive to the needs of each functional area.

2. To ensure there is a forum where the compliance officer can inform the committee on key compliance and industry developments relevant to the company and to request the advice of the compliance committee on key issues surrounding the compliance program.

One point that needs to be stressed is that the compliance committee is purely an advisory committee. It should not be empowered with authority over the compliance officer. Why? There is a common adage in Washington: "committee" equals "delay." You don't want to risk the delay of key compliance decisions unnecessarily because one person may want to delay that action. Those decisions are meant for the consideration of the GC and the CEO together with the compliance officer and, when necessary, for the board. At the same time, compliance committees are a valuable forum to build consensus and support. The principal objective of the committee is to build consensus for support of appropriate compliance initiatives and requirements and to make sure it is working effectively and is responsive to the needs of the business from an operational point of view.

COMPLIANCE OFFICER

When it comes to governance, the next key component is the position of the compliance officer; however, there is considerable variability in terms of what may work. There is no black-or-white answer or wrong way of doing this or that other than pros and cons and other considerations. The key question is, to whom should the compliance officer report?

Companies not under a CIA (discussed in the next section) often choose the compliance officer to report to the GC, or the GC also serves in that same capacity. The practical reasons for this are that first, compliance inherently starts with complying with the law, and second, it also reduces the number of direct reports to the CEO and associated costs of additional overhead.

Historically, the US government in the form of the OIG has recommended against this approach, to include in its most recent "General Compliance Program Guidance" issued in November 2023. Specifically, the guidance states, "The compliance officer should: report either directly to the CEO with direct independent access to the board, or to the board directly."[21] Doubling down on this point, the OIG continues and emphasizes in bold:

> *"Thus, the compliance officer should not lead or report to the entity's legal or financial functions, and should not provide the entity legal or financial advice or supervise anyone who does."*[22]

While the most recent compliance guidance from the OIG, like every previous one, is "voluntary," as we will discuss below, the OIG has mandated the compliance officer reporting relationship it recommends in the guidance to companies under a CIA.

CORPORATE INTEGRITY AGREEMENTS (CIAs)— GOVERNMENT-MANDATED STRUCTURE

Corporate integrity agreements, commonly referred to as CIAs, are agreements that are between the OIG-DHHS and a company accused

---

21 "General Compliance Program Guidance," US Department of Health and Human Services Office of Inspector General, November 2023, p. 37.

22 Ibid, p. 39.

of illegal conduct that agrees to a settlement with the DOJ. It's part of a broader criminal and/or civil settlement agreement with the DOJ. Instead of being barred from participating in federal healthcare programs as part of the settlement, companies are asked to agree to a CIA. CIAs are usually about five years in length, though they can be anywhere from three to, in some of the worst cases, seven years in length, as was the case with TAP's CIA. The CIAs mandate specific compliance program requirements and annual audits by an independent review organization. More complex CIAs may also require a compliance expert and/or a compliance monitor. All of these requirements demand a lot of resources. With strict deadlines and penalties for any misrepresentations or compliance failures, there is very little, if any, room for error.

For larger companies, CIA-related costs can run into millions of dollars—and it is obviously something you want to avoid.

These settlement agreements have, over time, provided a road map of the kinds of behavior and actions that companies should avoid. They have also provided valuable prescriptive templates for the specific compliance structures the OIG expects from and imposes upon companies under a CIA.

It is in CIAs that the OIG has required companies to appoint a compliance officer who either reports to the president/CEO with direct access to the board or reports directly to the board. The goal of the OIG is to ensure that the compliance officer has both real and apparent authority by vesting the role with sufficient credible independence and seniority.

From a practical perspective, most employees view the legal department's role as the primary defender of the company against allegations of impropriety or illegality. As we will see in the following actual case study, that can lead to hesitation or even fear in reporting concerns, where the perception may be that the fox is watching the henhouse.

CASE STUDY: PERCEPTION MATTERS

A chief compliance officer was hired after a company whistleblower reported concerns to the government that led to a federal investigation and subpoena. The publicly traded company had grown considerably through mergers and acquisitions and became the largest medical billing company in the country. This case involved a midlevel employee with a master's degree who believed they saw something improper but may not have had the total picture.

A midlevel executive in HR overheard the GC and the CEO talking about stock benefits for the two of them. He shared this in confidence with his boss, the VP of HR, but refused to make an official report to the compliance officer. The VP of HR then shared this situation with the chief compliance officer, relaying that a manager who worked for him had some serious concerns involving the GC and CEO but was afraid to come forward.

When brought to my attention, I thanked my HR colleague and asked him, "Do you know why this person is afraid?"

"Yes," he replied. "It's because it involves your boss, and he thinks there is nothing you can do."

"Do you mind if I speak to him?" I asked.

"No, but he may be fearful of saying anything," he said.

I went to the person's office and asked if I could speak with him alone. I said, "I understand you may have some questions or even concerns about a potential compliance matter but don't feel comfortable coming forward about. Do you mind if I ask you why?" He said, "Steve, I know you're a man of integrity, a Marine Corps officer, and someone who does what is right. With that said, I also know you are a man with a family to feed. My concern involves your boss, and you would be reporting on your boss and your boss's boss. I don't think you can do anything about it."

I responded, "First, thank you for sharing this. Let me reassure you that you have my word and commitment that if something improper is happening in this case, I will take it seriously and address it. If necessary and appropriate, I have authority to raise it to the board. If you have a compliance concern, it needs to be addressed. Second, if we need to act, we will. But also let me share with you that you may only have a piece of the total picture. That piece in isolation may seem inappropriate. But it is just one piece of a larger mosaic. Once we learn more and understand the total picture, it may not be an issue. Are you open to that possibility?" He said, "Yes." I said, "Great. Let's proceed, and we'll go to wherever the facts lead us and do what's right. You have my word." He breathed a sigh of relief, we shook hands, and then proceeded to discuss the details of his concerns. While on their face the facts he shared in isolation did indeed raise some serious questions, they did lead to other questions and other people, who, when interviewed, were able to provide the complete context.

As I had initially suspected, the HR person only had a small part of the big picture, and when I did my investigation, the CEO and GC were doing the right thing.

This case study illustrates that perception really does matter. Here, the perception was that, regardless of the otherwise credible integrity of the compliance officer, given his direct reporting relationship to the GC, he would be unable to do anything. There was no perceived credible independence, which created a chilling effect. Once, however, the person understood that the compliance officer also had access to the board, it provided a greater sense of security.

The bottom line is to whomever the compliance officer reports, employees should feel confident that any compliance issues or concerns will be addressed properly. Sharing the governance structure of the compliance program openly and transparently while also projecting the kind of strength of character and integrity on a personal level will inspire confidence in the credibility of the compliance program.

How to Build Proper Compliance Structure

Where do you start or how do you build a proper structure? Up until November 2023, with the release of the "General Compliance Program Guidance" by the OIG, in the pharmaceutical life sciences industry, the OIG's "Compliance Guidance for Pharmaceutical Manufacturers," released in 2003, has been the document from which to start. In that document it talks about what is now commonly referred to as the "Seven Elements."

THE SEVEN ELEMENTS OF AN EFFECTIVE COMPLIANCE PROGRAM

1. Implementing written policies, procedures, and standards of conduct.

2. Designating a compliance officer and compliance committee.

3. Conducting effective training and education.

4. Developing effective lines of communication.

5. Conducting internal monitoring and auditing.

6. Enforcing standards through well-publicized disciplinary guidelines.

7. Responding promptly to detected offenses and undertaking corrective action.

In the next chapter, we will address the Seven Elements.

CHAPTER 4

THE SEVEN ELEMENTS: DEFINING ESSENTIAL COMPLIANCE PRINCIPLES

People follow leaders by choice. Without trust, at best you get compliance.

—JESSE LYN STONER

When things get complicated, we are likely, as fallible people, to drop the ball. This is why I think spelling out the Seven Elements of Compliance is helpful. We establish the minimum requirements of a compliance program and why the elements of this framework are so important. The Seven Elements of Compliance provide the details for building a solid compliance program. It's not just about having a code of conduct or a chief compliance officer; it must be a specific process to be followed to be effective.

1. Implementing Written Policies, Procedures, and Standards of Conduct

The focus of this book is how to win with compliance as a force multiplier in your business by inspiring integrity to propel performance. However, at its core, compliance is still a legally driven process. Without written policies and procedures, any compliance program will fail. The centerpiece or cornerstone of a compliance program will be your code of business conduct and ethics. If you think of this code as your company's constitution, it will articulate your core values and principles while also reflecting key risks that will guide your company's and your employees' actions.

You will need to identify the core policies and procedures that we discussed in chapter 3, which include the importance of a risk assessment. Your carefully identified risks will guide the customization of your policies and procedures in your company.

2. Designating a Compliance Officer and Compliance Committee

Compliance is everyone's responsibility—it must be a part of your company's DNA. The compliance officer's role is to lead that effort by providing specific guidance, advice, and support to enable everyone in the company to be mindful of compliance and ensure the company stays in compliance. Everyone needs to be empowered to say something when they see an issue that needs to be addressed, is a risk, or could result in a future problem. In other words you want to build a culture where people recognize compliance issues and mention them right away without fear of reprisal.

That means creating a culture of integrity.

The compliance officer is the person who will help build your organization's commitment to compliance. Perhaps the number one quality of an effective compliance officer is credibility—someone who earns respect across the organization, from entry-level positions, new employees, and fresh-out-of-college summer interns to most senior executives and board members and everyone in between. A compliance officer should be able to communicate effectively and earn respect at all levels.

As with most executive positions, character, competence, and integrity are critical factors for success. Of course, with each organization, integrating the compliance person into the broader culture of the company is also important. For example, a young junior lawyer, fresh out of law school, likely won't work. Generally, it takes some time to have the full confidence to take the lead, especially if the C-suite and board are involved, and to feel comfortable pushing back—and knowing how to do it effectively—if there is an issue.

At the same time, on the other extreme, a retired senior executive may appear too detached for most employees to relate to. No candidate is perfect, but this is where companies need to be careful with whom they select and why.

In addition, perhaps the most important quality of a chief compliance officer is character and backbone combined with a refined sense of tact and diplomacy. For me, the latter took some time to develop. Marines are not especially known for the soft touch! Nevertheless, there is no better teacher than experience. When called upon, the chief compliance officer must make tough decisions at critical times, when the issues and their possible solutions are not necessarily crystal clear. That takes not only a strong backbone but also a sense of wisdom as to which battles are important to fight and which ones are not. At the end of the day, the chief compliance officer must be a leader and support the overarching mission of the company while at the same time have enough courage to raise the red flag when needed in the right way.

An effective compliance officer must be able to credibly, succinctly, and thoughtfully explain why there may be a concern and be a pragmatic problem solver who is adept at finding common ground between different points of view while creating workable and defensible solutions. At the same time, the compliance officer must balance business priorities with legal requirements and overarching public policy considerations.

A common question that has come up often over the years is, "Does the compliance officer need to be a lawyer?" The short answer is, "No—but it usually helps." First, for the obvious reasons, you are complying with laws, regulations, company policies, and procedures. The more you understand the law—how it is formed—the better prepared you are to implement and operationalize it.

On the other hand, the compliance officer does not supply legal advice as much as operational advice. What does that mean? It means they must translate legal advice into clear, actionable policies and procedures that enable the business to follow those procedures while implementing and complying with the Seven Elements.

3. Conducting Effective Training and Education

If people in the organization are not educated about compliance, then the most well-written policies in the world won't do you much good. When it comes to compliance training, there needs to be two kinds of training:

- Annual training on the code of business conduct and ethics and related policies and procedures

- Targeted training on specific issues as they develop within the industry or within the company

As with any kind of instruction, you want it to stick, so there are some basic rules and best practices about effective training and education that apply to compliance training. These include the following:

KNOW YOUR AUDIENCE

Whether you are speaking to entry-level salespeople or the board of directors, knowing their challenges, motivations, and fears, and being able to see the compliance world through their eyes, is a must. You must make the training relevant for them. You need to answer the question "why" behind the "what." In other words, why should I listen to this? What is in it for me? That is the question any salesperson must answer if they are going to get others to purchase their product. Selling compliance through training is no different. You also have to speak the language of the audience and know what is relevant to them from their perspective. The perspective of a board member is very different from that of an entry-level sales rep.

If you want to build a training program designed to stick, do your homework and provide real-life scenarios for your audience. Again, that differs depending on the level of the audience, as we will discuss in the example below.

UTILIZE HUMOR, BUT CAREFULLY

On one occasion, for a larger audience of two hundred to three hundred billing company owners who were at Disney World in Florida for the annual conference of the HBMA, I was doing a presentation about compliance programs and making the point that a compliance officer often wears many different hats.

As I was going through the various hats that I took out from behind the podium, I suggested that, at times, a compliance officer must be like a tough Marine but present in a formal way, so I used the Marine Corp dress blue cover. Other times, I said, the officer must be prepared for combat, and I pulled out a plastic combat helmet. Though I knew I looked ridiculous, it made everyone laugh. I was connecting with this audience and had their full attention.

As I moved toward the punch line of the presentation, I said, "If the OIG shows up, and you don't have the Seven Elements of a compliance program in place, this is how you will look to the OIG." I pulled out a Disney World hat that had the Goofy snout and ears hanging over my head. I looked, well, you guessed it, "Goofy," and everyone cracked up laughing. They had fun while understanding my self-deprecating humor to make a serious, heavy subject a bit lighter.

I received many compliments from the OIG counsel who was with me on stage and from many audience members—all of whom were potential clients! Clearly, it was a successful speech—straight out of Disney!

Fast-forward to three months later, when I was invited to present to a pharmaceutical advisory board of serious-minded (and, as it turned out, humorless) physicians in Jacksonville, Florida. In retrospect, I should have realized just how opposite the circumstances were at this venue compared with the HBMA meeting. Here, we were at the posh Ritz-Carlton resort in Jacksonville, Florida. (This was in the late 1990s, before the TAP case and the ensuing pharmaceutical sales and marketing reforms.) Instead of presenting to two hundred or three hundred people, I had about fifteen people in the room, who were ready to get down to business.

The mistake I made was that I presented the same routine as I did at Disney World with the different hats. But instead of laughs, chuckles, and applause, I faced a room full of silence, with elderly gray-haired physicians, dressed in sport coats, a few wearing bow ties, with grim faces and folded arms. Back then, nearly thirty years ago, I must have come across as this young punk, smart-alecky lawyer with a Washington background speaking to them about something they hated—legal compliance requirements. To add insult to injury, I literally used the same "Goofy" routine ... and to my later chagrin, it was being videotaped! Well, needless to say, I was a total bomb with this audience. The one collective laugh I did achieve is when we all went out on a chartered fishing excursion, and the one lawyer on the boat full of doctors caught ... you guessed it ... a shark and threw it back "out of professional courtesy"! But the painful lesson I learned that day and, one I have never forgotten, is that just because one presentation works with one audience doesn't mean it will work with another. The bottom line is whatever hat you wear, it needs to fit the occasion. Particularly for a serious subject such as compliance, you can use humor to help disarm the audience *where appropriate* and make them more receptive to your message. But always *read the room and adjust to it.*

IMPLEMENT THE BEST TRAINING

When it comes to effective training, don't rely on any one form; have a mix. Depending on the company's size and budget, you will need to determine the best mix among the following three types to consider:

- Live training: in-person or virtual using a platform such as Zoom or Teams

- Technical computer based

- Prerecorded training

I have found that by far the most effective training is live in-person training; it is the most interactive and is best at triggering the senses such as sight, hearing, and connecting with people's emotions. However, given the logistical challenges in many organizations today, especially in a virtual world, that can be difficult to pull off. Live virtual training, such as those on Zoom, can be very effective as well, but you better do test runs to make sure you avoid technical problems, which can be very disruptive, annoying, and frustrating for all. Since the COVID-19 pandemic, we've learned how to improve online training, and people are more open to learning that. For example, a major global online learning platform reported that during the pandemic, over twenty million new learners registered for their courses.[23] The least effective training is death by PowerPoint. Slides dryly presented by a person who is not passionate about the topic may even be worse than a sign-and-read option, where you don't have the numbing, negative effect of a boring person.

Regardless, injecting passion and energy every time you present is how you make compliance training memorable, engaging, and effective.

DOCUMENT EVERYTHING

One basic rule of training is that if it is not documented, it is not done. This rule applies to compliance generally as well, not just training attendance. People need to be tested, and the test should not be just memorization but also how they can find the right answer within the company's compliance documents. An open-book test that gives people the opportunity to find answers to true-life situations within

---

23   "These 3 Charts Show the Global Growth in Online Learning," World Economic Forum, January 27, 2022, https://www.weforum.org/agenda/2022/01/online-learning-courses-reskill-skills-gap/.

the code of conduct gives them practice in what you expect of them day-to-day, after the training is completed. Rote memorization does not demonstrate knowledge. Instead, knowing how to solve a novel problem—knowing where to go for answers—is far more important.

4. Developing Effective Lines of Communication

The fourth of the Seven Elements is developing effective lines of communication, and this necessarily encompasses many different methods. However, when it comes to communication, many companies miss the opportunity to brand their compliance program with a seal, logo, or something distinctive and memorable. I first wrote a chapter for LexisNexis on marketing a compliance program in 2008, titled "Marketing the Compliance Program Internally," and I have been invited to update it ever since. (See chapter 25, volume 1 of the LexisNexis *Corporate Compliance Practice Guide: The Next Generation of Compliance*, edited by Carole Basri, Release 16.)

The branding we created for TAP Pharmaceuticals was called "Acting on Our Values" (AOV).

*TAP Compliance branding with Acting on Our Values
logo and booth at national sales meeting*

I pioneered this concept. Necessity is indeed the mother of invention. I remember looking around at the TAP sales force. They were all relatively young, most in their mid- to late twenties. As is common in pharmaceutical sales, these folks were very attractive, good-looking athletes, former military guys, beauty pageant winners, and models. As I learned, this was by design. Most do not have chemistry or biology degrees. Some do. Certainly, some of the better ones do. And increasingly, there is greater demand for scientifically educated sales reps, as the products are getting increasingly scientifically complex. But I can tell you from firsthand, direct experience for over twenty years that the primary emphasis is on the ability of the salesperson to connect with another person, having the "it factor," the likability factor versus technical knowledge. I quickly realized at the time that a typical legal, corporate presentation on compliance would fall on deaf ears. I thought to myself, "This compliance stuff is just too damn dry and boring. It's black-and-white legal pages written by lawyers, and these sales folks' eyes are going to gloss over in thirty seconds. We need to do something else."

Perhaps because of my athletic and military experiences, and as a history buff, I knew that every country, every government and military organization creates seals and symbols that convey a sense of gravitas, convey a sense of identity, and convey a sense of meaning of what these organizations represent. I had seen it in Washington, DC, on the brass signage outside of embassies, the Pentagon, and scientific organizations. In practice, it creates a sense of identity and pride for members of these organizations.

In essence, it's branding, much like branding a product. It's giving dimensions to a concept. I did not want the idea of compliance to be dismissed as a "flavor of the month" corporate initiative. We gave it a lot of thought—and the results were great.

It is important, whatever your communication strategy, that it not go over people's heads. You want your message to "stick." Weaving the principles, values, and mission of the company into the DNA of compliance is important and vice versa. People tend to remember images much more easily than words. Utilize the five "R's" of effective branding:

- Raison d'être

- Reputation

- Relevance

- Recognition

- Repetition[24]

At TAP we created a seal that had at its center hands lifting and supporting "TAP" in the midst of a radiating sun, symbolizing that it is the people of TAP that will bring it success. This image is framed in

---

24   David A. Shore, *The Trust Crisis in Healthcare* (Oxford: Oxford University Press, 2007), 149–153.

a circle with "Ethics & Compliance" at the top and the Latin phrase "Aequis Ponderibus Librans" at the bottom, which translates literally to "balancing with equal weight" or, in other words, striking the right balance. Finally, as a sign of equilibrium, we have the words, "Acting on Our Values" across the center to show how we strike that right balance.

The TAP Compliance Department Seal

The taglines "Acting on Our Values" and "Striking the Right Balance" were specifically chosen for TAP as a way to send a clear message that actions driven by values are what mattered and that Ethics & Compliance was tempered by the realization for the need for balance and equilibrium. We wanted to allay what is usually the biggest fear of executives and board members—that the compliance department will be the "Just Say No" department. Again, the whole concept was to symbolize balance, reasonableness, and the idea that people taking action based on shared values will lift TAP to success. The focus was to brand the compliance program as a key positive and reasonable element of the company's future business success.

The TAP Acting on Our Values Award
(This one was presented to me from my team on my
last day at TAP.)

To recognize positive compliance contributions and to associate compliance with positive rewards, we also created the Acting on Our Values Award. The president of TAP and I presented this award at the national sales meeting to recipients in each region of the country nominated by their managers.

This award and seal (i.e., the AOV brand) signaled to everybody that the company is a serious company of integrity, where everyone is expected to lead by example and walking the talk. Our goal was to package this in a very sincere way to make clear we are all about helping our patients have a better life. That's why we are here—all of us in life sciences. And whether we're a first-year intern at a college, a senior scientist, an experienced sales rep, an entry-level sales rep, or an administrative assistant, we are all there for the same reason—and we are proud to be a part of such a company. That's one of the things they really teach you in the Marines. We want to instill in everyone a sense of pride of who you are and what you represent.

The Marine Corps Seal
The few, the proud, the Marines

I have found that as an internal matter, some companies prevent different functions within the company, such as a compliance department, from developing their own brand within the company. However, many do allow it, and where possible, I strongly recommend it. The reason a brand is so important is because it gives dimension and meaning to something that is otherwise very generic and loaded with negative connotation. As with any effective product brand, an effective brand triggers an instant reflexive response as to what the brand signifies and the meaning behind it. The AOV logo became instantly recognized by all levels of employees to symbolize integrity, action, collaboration, and success.

Another example of using branding to associate compliance with positive messages was the following campaign created for Warner

Chilcott. You may recall from an earlier chapter that we turned the existing company logo consisting of the letters WC into a tagline of "Winning with Compliance."

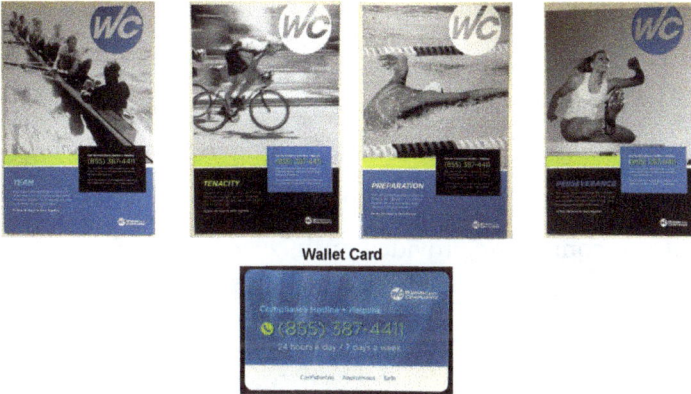

BRANDING AND RAISING AWARENESS: HOTLINE + HELPLINE PROMOTION

"To Win, We Need to Work Together!"

Wallet Card

Another positive incentive we created at TAP was incorporating compliance into executive bonus calculations—compliance was being poured into the lifeblood of the company. If you are going to walk the talk, it should be about the bottom line as well.

YOUR COMMUNICATIONS STRATEGY

After developing a brand, a whole communications strategy should next be employed, whether it is through annual training or targeted training that affords the opportunity to interact through sales meetings.

One way we did this was to create booths at conferences or meetings that allowed people to interact with me as the compliance officer and my team; this draws people in and gives them opportunities to meet each person within the compliance department. This is a great way to humanize compliance and make it more approachable so when employees and the compliance officer are in the field, people won't be afraid to ask questions. Compliance officers become human, not just the feared "compliance man" (or woman).

One of the most creative things we did at TAP Pharmaceuticals's conference was an interactive game called "Rocked or Shocked." Sales teams would be pitted against each other in a contest to see which team could rack up the highest number of points by correctly answering the most compliance-related questions. After a countdown to start the game, the sole contestant up at bat would then see the first of ten questions in sixty seconds. An animated, simulated sales rep would appear on flat screen as loud rock 'n' roll music blasted from the speakers to increase the pressure. To further enhance the experience, if the contestant provided an incorrect answer, the animated sales rep would get "shocked" on screen and yell out, "Hey, you need to do better, man!" Contestants could have their sales teammates stand around and shout out what they thought was the right answer. But only the contestant at the console could decide which answer to select. The questions were randomly selected from a pool of previously prepared questions, so no two contestants ever had the exact same mix of questions. The winning team was announced at the end of the meeting and received a large Stanley Cup–like trophy and could proudly display it as the reigning Compliance Champions until the next year's contest. Sound silly? It worked for Abbott Labs, Walmart, Goldman Sachs, and other companies that purchased and employed this game we created with our vendor. The real kicker in all of this is the TAP Compliance Department and TAP actually generated revenue for the company by receiving royalties for every sale of the game! This added real truth to the other tagline we used: "Good Compliance *Is* Good Business!"

Bottom line: People can't comply with what they can't remember. Whether it is the visuals of an award, an appropriate humorous story, a fun game, or a pneumonic device, remembering the principles of compliance is essential, so use all the tools and communication techniques at your disposal to connect with your target audiences, always tailoring your technique to that audience.

A woman playing the "Get Rocked or Shocked" Compliance contest.

BE *BOLD* AND THINK DIFFERENT

The real message here is find ways to engage your audience so that you challenge their preconceptions and show them that compliance can be different from what they expected. I used the principle of jiujitsu— use the weight of your opponent against itself. Here, the opponent was the perception of commercial sales and marketing professionals that compliance was essentially bad for business, that it was a "sales inhibitor." I showed it was exactly the opposite and used effective sales and marketing techniques to "sell" compliance to sales and marketing professionals. It worked!

Good marketing professionals know you win people over by first winning their trust, seeing them as people, and developing a human rapport. As the bond of respect and trust strengthens between people, so, too, does the confidence to share thoughts and ideas and, perhaps at the most mature level, concerns. That is the relationship evolution that should and can progress with a compliance program. At the end of the day, you want people to have enough trust so that they can turn to a compliance officer to ask a question, to share a concern as opposed to turning away or not discussing an issue. This is why communications as the fourth element of a compliance program is often thought of as *the most important* of the Seven Elements. It is the linchpin that, if effective, yields the outcomes you want from an effective compliance program. You must connect with your audience. How you do that really matters.

5. Conducting Internal Monitoring and Auditing

Monitoring and auditing are not the same. **Monitoring** is keeping your finger on the pulse of the company in present, real time. **Auditing** is a backward look in time of past events and activities to see if people are compliant with the rules, regulations, policies, and procedures. Auditing is done through a diligent and careful review of relevant materials that include various records, documentation, and interview results.

MONITORING WITH A MISSION

Like the word "compliance," "monitoring" does not usually conjure up a positive image. Too often it is framed as an exercise in finding mistakes, which becomes perceived as a game of "Gotcha!"

Instead, monitoring should be about establishing mutual trust. If a compliance issue is found, it should be treated as a golden moment to mentor, educate, and find solutions to prevent it in the future. As a leader, this is an opportunity to get in touch with real-world circumstances and, while doing so, learn, inspire, and motivate how to sell both ethically and effectively. Live, in-person field monitoring is how you keep your finger on the pulse of what's happening.

COVID-19 challenged the life sciences industry in many ways to ensure employee well-being, supply of products required, business continuity, and unwavering innovation. While virtual appointments are not going away, the natural excitement of meeting in person again, combined with the enormous pressure salespeople face to make deals and rekindle relationships, makes it the right time to plan for field monitoring. A competitive atmosphere, combined with greater risks and stricter enforcement, indicates that it is time to rethink how field monitoring will be deployed, executed, and by whom.

Certainly, from a compliance perspective, you need to know and identify if a sales call is being conducted improperly. However, here's that corner again—ethics and integrity. Monitoring ensures your company's ethics are lived. Just as importantly, field monitoring creates an opportunity to inspire and motivate your sales team to comply for the right reasons. It's an opportunity to build trust so that you can also learn from individual sales reps about the real- world compliance risks that they encounter. Whether it's virtual or in person, a hybrid monitoring model that considers both digital and face-to-face meetings will likely be the most effective model in the foreseeable future.

From a salesperson's perspective, having a stranger with the task of "compliance monitor" follow you around for eight to ten hours can be intimidating and downright scary. Believe me, I understand. (I would not want a stranger following me around either—even though I know the importance of it.) People have been known to have sleepless nights before meeting their assigned monitor. Concerns can be exacerbated by a fear that the compliance officer does not understand the business of the organization or even how business is done in the real world. It's important to recognize the reality of this genuine fear factor.

However, it does not have to be this scary. First, getting the right person to conduct your monitoring is key. The ideal seasoned compliance professional will approach monitoring more as a coach or mentor. Listening actively, observing, and providing thoughtful feedback that answers the why behind the what of compliance communicates mutual respect and generates value. That is how you win trust. An experienced field monitor will reinforce that they're there to understand challenges and help find solutions that tie compliance back to the core values and healthcare mission of the company. I may be a Marine, but the drill sergeant approach won't work.

Core values are lived when they have personal meaning. For me, integrity is just an essential element in my makeup. I believe a person's word is their bond. Core values remain, no matter the circumstances. At the first time of difficulty, that value cannot just vanish. I try to keep my word, even when it's under challenging circumstances.

In corporate America core values are what support the vision, shape the culture, and reflect what a company values in their work. They are the essence of the company's identity, principles, and beliefs. Many companies focus on the technical competencies but forget that the underlying competencies that make their company run smoothly are core values and ethics. Establishing strong core values provides internal and external advantages from decision-making to educating consumers and clarifying the identity of the company, and they can become primary recruiting and retention tools.

When field monitors can tie compliance to core values, compliance becomes meaningful. Another positive way to think about the role of field monitors is as "compliance ambassadors." Salespeople have tough jobs. Most are good people who want to do their work well, but they are under a lot of pressure. They have limited time to get their message out and connect with customers, who are hard to book, and working over Zoom has been a struggle for us all. Everyone is "Zoomed" out, to say the least.

While we all know that lavish steak dinners and exotic trips are out of bounds, making smaller offerings that test boundaries can be tough to resist. An experienced field monitor can explain the difference between an appropriate modest lunch and an inappropriate extravagant dinner. Regulations at the state, local, and country levels, combined with the need to track healthcare providers, mean life science organizations need a disciplined approach to manage enterprise-wide meeting and event programs. By observing tactics and behaviors, experienced monitors can give feedback—tying it to integrity—and nip bad habits in the bud as trusted compliance coaches and mentors. Again, here is an opportunity to inspire integrity, to foster compliance, and to create a win-win-win outcome—a win for the sales rep, a win for the company, and a win for the customer.

By contrast, assigning a young, inexperienced monitor who stays silent, takes notes, and completes a monitoring checklist only reinforces the fear factor of compliance. Compliance officers who deploy the right monitors into the field and factor this into their strategic plans set their salespeople up for success by keeping them safe from risks. Field monitoring is less about identifying or detecting bad practices (which, if they are occurring, you certainly must do) and more about *preventing* them. Monitoring should be used as an opportunity for coachable moments, constructive feedback, and reinforcing a job well done.

The right monitor adds value by representing you in the field as your ambassador, who can win trust and inspire compliance and integrity on your behalf (and who is savvy enough to recognize BS when they see and hear it). Conducting field monitoring in this realistic, pragmatic, and positive manner will help you prevent misconduct, support your sales team, and unleash their skills, propelling performance in the process.

MONITORING ELECTRONIC DOCUMENTATION

Increasingly, the DOJ has emphasized the importance of data analytics in modern, effective compliance programs. In the most recent DOJ guidance on the evaluation of compliance programs, the DOJ writes, "Do compliance and control personnel have sufficient direct or indirect access to relevant sources of data to allow for timely and effective monitoring and/or testing of policies, controls, and transactions?"[25]

By taking a sample of emails or expense reports from the company's computer system, you can look for key words and identify content that may trigger questions or concerns.

Since the transformational changes of COVID-19 age, today, it is not uncommon for a compliance officer to use remote monitoring through Zoom, where the compliance officer can attend an advisory board meeting, listen in, see how the program is being conducted, and take notes. Going forward, the advantages of time and cost of conducting events remotely will remain, suggesting that monitoring will include both remote and in-person monitoring into the foreseeable future.

---

25   US Department of Justice Criminal Division, "Evaluation of Corporate Compliance Programs," updated March 2023, p. 11.

AUDITING

Auditing is a look back at time that includes past events to make sure they were conducted in compliance with laws and regulations. Generally, audits are done annually or semiannually depending on how large the organization is. Auditing includes interviewing key individuals and personnel, focusing on commercial activities such as leaders of the commercial team, and reviewing key documents such as the following:

- Expense reports of any kind

- Contracts

- Speaker agreements

- Attendance documents of different events and who partici-pated in a program

An audit is a comprehensive review of past activities within a defined time frame to verify that the company and its employees are following the established policies and procedures of the compliance program when conducting activities that the government may have identified as high risk, such as speaker programs and advisory boards, or any time there is a transfer of value between the company and an HCP.

For example, on November 16, 2020, the OIG issued a Special Fraud Alert regarding speaker programs in the healthcare industry. This was the first Special Fraud Alert since 2014 and only the fourth issued in the past two decades. Only eleven had ever been announced since they began in 1994. This was clearly a significant event and a clear warning from the OIG to the industry about the risks and concerns the OIG has with conducting speaker programs.

Recently, drug and device companies had reported paying nearly $2 billion to HCPs for speaker-related programs. The OIG had taken note and expressed its significant concerns about such remunerations and the value of these programs. The specific concern was that these programs serviced as improper inducements to prescribe FDA-approved products that were reimbursed by federal healthcare programs. In the eyes of the OIG, if that intent is present, both the company and the HCPs may be subject to possible enforcement actions.

It's important to note that this Special Fraud Alert is not intended to discourage meaningful HCP training and education. However, it does highlight certain inherent risks of remuneration related to speaker programs. As a result drug and device companies, as well as HCPs, should carefully consider the risks when assessing whether to offer, pay, solicit, or receive remuneration related to speaker programs.

Understanding the difference between what's considered ethical and what's suspect is critical to running a successful speaker program. The illustrative list below provides some key examples of what will likely raise concerns with the OIG. The presence or absence of any one of these factors is not the only determination of whether a particular program would be suspect under the Anti-Kickback Statute, but they're certainly all worth your attention and thoughtful consideration.

Lack of Substance. A company that sponsors speaker programs where little or no substantive information is presented is going to raise some flags. Programs should be specifically focused on drugs and devices and news and innovations within the industry.

Fancy Food and Drink. If you're serving alcohol, especially if it's free, or a lavish meal, you might catch the attention of the OIG. Keep food and beverage costs modest. It's an industry event, not a party.

Location, Location, Location. If your program is being held at a venue that seems more fun than work oriented, reconsider the place. The setting should be conducive to the exchange of educational information. Think conference rooms, not restaurants or entertainment and sports centers.

No Recent Updates to Product. Sponsoring multiple programs on the same topic or product, especially if there have been no recent or relevant updates to it, is frowned upon. Likewise, if a significant period has passed with no new medical or scientific information and/or it hasn't been recently FDA approved, holding a speaker program would be risky. To be safe, time programs to coincide with substantial changes and announcements about your products or research.

Attending Repeat Programming. When healthcare providers attend multiple programs on the same or closely related topics, it raises a red flag. This can include being a repeat attendee and/or speaker at multiple programs.

Including Nonrelevant Guests. Individuals who don't have a legitimate business reason to attend a program should be left off the guest list. To meet the OIG's guidelines, friends, significant others, and family members of speakers or attendees should stay at home. The same goes for employees, medical professionals, and other staff who would not directly benefit from the program's information.

Hiring Speakers Based on Potential (or Past) Revenue. Your company's sales and marketing teams should not influence the selection of speakers (or attendees). Hiring talent or identifying participants based on prior or potential revenue is considered bad form by the OIG.

Paying Speakers Too Much. Paying or otherwise compensating HCP speakers more than the fair market value (FMV) for their services is another warning sign. Avoid this by paying fairly but within reasonable parameters. It's best to get an independent FMV expert who can provide the current FMV data for specific physician therapeutic specialties by tiers affected by factors, such as years of experience, number of academic publications, geographic area, etc.

With the recent Special Fraud Alert, trends toward stricter compliance regulations, and the likely tendency of current and future administrations to be more skeptical of industry motivations, it's more important than ever to make sure your compliance program is in order. Regardless of who wins the next presidential election, this will continue to be a hot topic, as the "war on healthcare fraud," as first announced in the early 1990s under President Clinton's administration, has continued for over thirty years under every administration since, regardless of which political party was in office.

So be prepared and stay prepared. Regardless of who sits in the Oval Office, the crackdown on healthcare fraud and abuse will continue. So inspiring integrity and finding a way to win with compliance will remain essential to be able to compete and win aggressively in the marketplace.

APPEARANCES MATTER

One example comes to mind with regard to appearances and discrediting circumstances. This was for a speaker program that I observed as a retained compliance consultant conducting field monitoring for a medical device company. The medical device company asked me to attend this speaker program at a restaurant literally advertised as the newest and best steakhouse in Chicago. Even though the sales rep who organized this program was trained by his company to provide only "modest meals" in compliance with the PhRMA Code, he held the program at this brand-new "buzzy" place with loud music thumping in the background and five-star reviews. We could hardly hear one another with the hum of the bar right next door, even though we were in a private dining room that was partitioned only with sliding curtains.

Attendees enjoyed an exceptional (a.k.a. pricey) steak dinner with an excellent speaker. From a substantive content perspective, the program could not have been better. The speaker was a well-respected expert in his field … but you could hardly hear him! In addition, many of the young residents who were in attendance had heard all this content before and openly expressed excitement about this latest venue. Talk about red flags! Obviously, it is important to present new educational content at a venue that is conducive to an educational presentation to new guests. Having repeat people come to the same event that ends up being a party is exactly what the OIG warns against. The sales rep who organized the dinner was a young, energetic guy, full of a can-do attitude, but he couldn't have gotten the venue more wrong, and he put the company, and all who attended, at risk.

By contrast, another group with the same company went to a more suburban restaurant that had a separate conference room set up like a classroom for the doctors, and a medical school professor was the speaker. After having a nice meal, we could see the screen perfectly, and as he continued to speak, the professor was asking questions that I knew the answers to, but the resident doctors did not. Shocked that they didn't know the answers to the questions, all I could think at that moment was, "I hope I don't get these guys as one of my doctors in the future!" Still, we were all learning. The quality of the program was excellent, and the venue made all the difference in the world in terms of the credibility of the program.

On another occasion that involved a field ride in Tucson, Arizona, for a pharmaceutical company, a sales rep in that region set up a breakfast meeting, complete with sign-in sheets and visual aids for a large medical practice. She was organized and professional, and she properly engaged each person with appropriate product information. The owner of the medical practice arrived about thirty minutes late with two large Siberian huskies and asked to have them fed with the scrambled eggs from breakfast.

The physician, in his late sixties and very sure of himself, said to the sales rep, "Things look good. How's it going?"

"Very well," she said and turned to introduce me. "This is Steve from our home office."

"Good morning," I said, shaking his hand. "I am here to make sure things are going well from a compliance perspective."

Without blinking an eye, he then said as he turned to face the sales rep, "Let me ask this young lady, are you having an advisory board meeting in Maui?"

"Sir ... I don't know," she replied, taken a bit off guard by the directness of his solicitation. "We are here to help you determine whether our product can help any of your patients' unmet medical needs."

"Well, I guess I'm not going to prescribe your product then," he said rather abruptly.

"Well, sir," I said to him, "we hold advisory board meetings when necessary, and our purpose here today is to make sure you have the right information to make the right independent medical decision for your patients."

"Okay, thank you very much," he said as he turned to walk out. "Goodbye."

The sales rep looked at me, eyes wide, and said, "I can't believe that just happened."

"Well," I said, "you read about this all the time, and we just witnessed it live and in person. This guy was looking for an all-expenses-paid trip to Maui from your company under the guise of serving on the advisory board. Talk about a blatant example of a potential kickback! You kept your cool and responded appropriately to him. Well done."

6. Enforcing Standards through Well-Publicized Disciplinary Guidelines

When the facts show that a violation has occurred, first and foremost, appropriate consequences must ensue, and discipline must be taken. Otherwise, all the policies, procedures, communications, and auditing are worthless. It will be a toothless, ineffective compliance program, both from an internal employee perspective and from an external OIG and DOJ perspective. For many executives, discipline is the toughest part of the compliance program and is often especially hard for executives in smaller companies who often feel like the head of one big family. When everyone knows everyone and has built something from the ground up that's successful, it can be hard to discipline anyone.

Invariably, there are people who cross limits, push the rules, and continue to do that in spite of warnings. All of the effort in making sure things are done properly to avoid discipline boils down to having to make a choice in order to have an effective program. Discipline needs to be consistent, proportional, and well documented. Once disciplinary action is taken, it sends a perceptible tremor throughout the company, indicating that boundaries are enforced. We address this in greater detail in the seventh and final element of the compliance framework.

7. Responding Promptly to Detected Offenses and Undertaking Corrective Action

As with anything in life, it is important to learn from your experiences, whether they are positive or negative. This means taking disciplinary action for small infractions is important because it ensures that bigger offenses are less likely to occur. This last element is about understanding that the standard of compliance is not about perfection but ultimately prevention. When mistakes have been made, you have to learn from the experience and put in place measures that will prevent those mistakes from occurring again.

Emphasize that if you have a series of inappropriate speaker programs, for example, you discipline the people who are in violation of your policies and do the following:

- Issue targeted training.

- Revise policies.

- Address specifics.

- Review inappropriate venues.

In other words make sure that everyone in your company understands the importance of these violations and put in place measures to prevent offenses from reoccurring. As a compliance officer, you often will find yourself in no-win situations, confronted with seemingly impossible decisions. As a corporate leader, your integrity may be tested when everyone in the company may be under extreme pressure to meet very aggressive goals … and something goes very wrong. You know this team, you like this team, and your gut tells you that no one on this team is a crook. Yet you know that while no one may have a dishonest intent, someone is and must be accountable. That person, in fact, may have to be you. But someone needs to stand up and take responsibility. The key to success then is to prevent this nightmare scenario from ever occurring. That is why in the Marines, they teach the five P's—Proper Preparation Prevents Poor Performance. Weaving compliance into the commercial and corporate DNA in a way that inspires integrity and reinforces teamwork and collaboration by cultivating a culture of trust and respect is how you will win with compliance and propel performance.

TRUTH OR CONSEQUENCES

I think it's helpful to offer some examples of case scenarios that include a regulator's thought process by understanding the use of your compliance information (or lack thereof) to determine consequences. One way to engage everyone in compliance is to play the game *Truth or Consequences* by asking "What would you do?" in specific situations related to compliance. This exercise helps create positive thought patterns to determine the best course of action in a variety of compliance situations.

At different times in my career, I found myself in the middle of opposing forces I had to deal with to make a choice. No matter what choice I made, there were negative consequences. I made my decisions by creating a checklist of the pros and cons of a situation. When you're under pressure to make a tough decision, it's useful to have a clear, distilled checklist to guide you through the decision-making process, knowing the strict rules of an effective compliance program. The list below offers an orderly, systematic approach to analyzing any compliance issue.

1. **First, Stop and Think.** Too often, people make a rash decision or rush into something unethical before they fully realize the consequences.

2. **Clarify Goals.** Boil complex goals down to the mission. Keep that top of mind.

3. **Determine Facts.** Remember my earlier example of the GC and CEO of a company perhaps engaging in perceived misconduct? It was right for the whistleblower

to come forward and share his concerns. My mission then was to determine the facts.

4. **Develop Options.** Never feel backed into a corner. Explore options in all situations.

5. **Consider Consequences.** I hope this entire book serves as a testament to readers that the consequences of not having a proper compliance program are myriad. Consequences accompany every choice we make, and the consequences of any ethical dilemma must always be considered.

6. **Choose, Monitor, Modify.** Decisions in compliance are rarely "the end." Instead, compliance is an ongoing process of making ethical, legal choices; monitoring activities; and revisiting and modifying policies, training, and communications as needed.

Sometimes What's Right and What's Wrong Is Clear

I also want to take a moment here to discuss the line in the sand. Yes, the steps above are imperative to decisions, the elements are pillars of compliance, but there is also another fundamental piece to compliance. At some point the fog of gray lifts, and what is left may become a crystal clear line between what makes sense and what does not.

Without taking a political stance one way or the other, what comes to mind are protests. In recent years university deans and leaders of cities around the United States have had to make decisions on student protests. The right to free speech is a protected right under the First Amendment of the Constitution. Legal protests are protected free speech. But—and as a "compliance guy," here's my caveat—when protests turn criminal, such as when students threaten other students or university employees with physical harm, destroy property, or disrupt or prevent the use of university facilities, including attending classes that students and their families have often paid tens of thousands of dollars to attend at great sacrifice, well, that's not gray. That's simply illegal and even criminal conduct that are clearly prohibited by both university regulations and codes of conduct, as well as by local laws and regulations. As an alumnus of Columbia University, I watched in dismay at the university's incremental, hand-wringing response to the Palestinian protests in the spring of 2024. They got compliance wrong and, by doing so, incited foreseeable and unnecessary further escalation of the tense situation. In short, the university's perceived and actual weakness in the face of aggressive illegal behavior led to more and even worse illegal behavior that culminated in the forceful occupation of Hamilton Hall. As I wrote at the time, this was Chamberlain-esque behavior. They tried to appease aggression, and as World War II and history have taught us, appeasing aggression begets more aggression.

The lesson here is that the compliance decision, in fact, may be clear and easy; enforcing it, however, may be politically unpopular and difficult but necessary to serve in the best interests of the larger community. So don't overcomplicate compliance when it is neither complex nor gray.

Now that we have examined the Seven Elements of a compliance program, we need to discuss one of the newer dilemmas compliance officers and organizations must face. In the modern era, where data is king (or queen) and companies are handling unimaginable masses of it, and with proprietary and personal data in the crosshairs of hackers and nefarious actors, *privacy* is part of the new compliance frontier, especially in healthcare and the life sciences.

CHAPTER 5:

PRIVACY: THE NEW COMPLIANCE OF LIFE SCIENCES

I believe in the men who take the next step; not those who theorize about the 200th step ... Reform is the antidote to revolution.

—THEODORE ROOSEVELT

n 2020 cyberagencies in the United Kingdom and Canada released a statement to the effect that if COVID-19 vaccine developments were hacked, it would set back the pharmaceutical industries' efforts to develop a vaccine.[26] Privacy in the life sciences and pharmaceuticals sector is paramount because of the sensitive nature of the personal healthcare data involved and the ethical implications associated with its use. This industry handles vast amounts of personal health information, genetic data, and proprietary research findings, all of which require stringent protection to maintain trust and ensure compliance with regulatory standards. The confidentiality of patient data is not only a legal obligation under frameworks such as Health

---

26   John Curran, "Cisa's Corman Warns Covid Vaccine Hacks Could Endanger Millions," MeriTalk.com, September 17, 2020, https://www.meritalk.com/articles/cisas-corman-warns-covid-vaccine-hacks-could-endanger-millions/.

Insurance Portability and Accountability Act (HIPAA) and General Data Protection Regulation (GDPR) but also a moral imperative to safeguard individual rights and prevent misuse. In research and development, the protection of intellectual property is critical for fostering innovation and ensuring that the benefits of new discoveries reach the public while securing commercial interests. Furthermore, breaches of privacy can lead to significant harm, including identity theft, discrimination, and financial loss, as well as reputational damage to organizations involved. Ensuring robust privacy measures in life sciences and pharmaceuticals is also crucial for fostering public confidence in scientific research, encouraging participation in clinical trials, and facilitating the responsible sharing of data for advancing medical knowledge.

As technology evolves and data analytics play an increasingly central role in healthcare, the challenge of maintaining privacy becomes more complex, necessitating continuous advancements in data security practices. Thus, the importance of privacy in this field cannot be overstated, as it underpins the ethical and effective advancement of medical science and the protection of individual and collective well-being.

Privacy is the new compliance for the life sciences industry.

A New Era of Compliance Risks

The TAP Settlement drew a clear line between how the life sciences industry handled compliance pre- and post-2001. More recently, COVID-19 affected life sciences in the same dramatic way. The pandemic was a catalyst for new compliance issues in ways and to a magnitude that no one could have foreseen. As we've all been forced into a world of chronic electronic communications, we are also required to rely on the security of these platforms. This includes not just talking but also transmitting documents and sharing sensitive information. It also includes commercial operations, such as selling.

Privacy and data security issues have always existed, but they are now magnified because of additional dependency and risks. Again, *privacy is the new compliance.* It has become a central component that must be integrated into any modern compliance program.

A shift in legislation regarding healthcare and privacy is compounding these risks. Consumer-oriented laws, which have already taken hold in Europe, are trickling into the United States. These requirements go beyond HIPAA, informing and enabling consumers to make decisions about what information is collected, by whom, and whether to opt out. The California Privacy Rights Act follows Europe's requirement for an opt-out provision for consumers.

Several other states have now enacted similar legislation. (See table on the next page.) Given the risks driving this new legislation and the political pressures and priorities of both parties, there's an increasing likelihood that momentous new bipartisan privacy legislation will be enacted soon. In short, we're on the threshold of a new age of legislation that will require new implementation. The onus of regulations will not decline. As new technologies, such as artificial intelligence, come to the forefront, they, too, will need regulatory frameworks. It grows ever more complex.

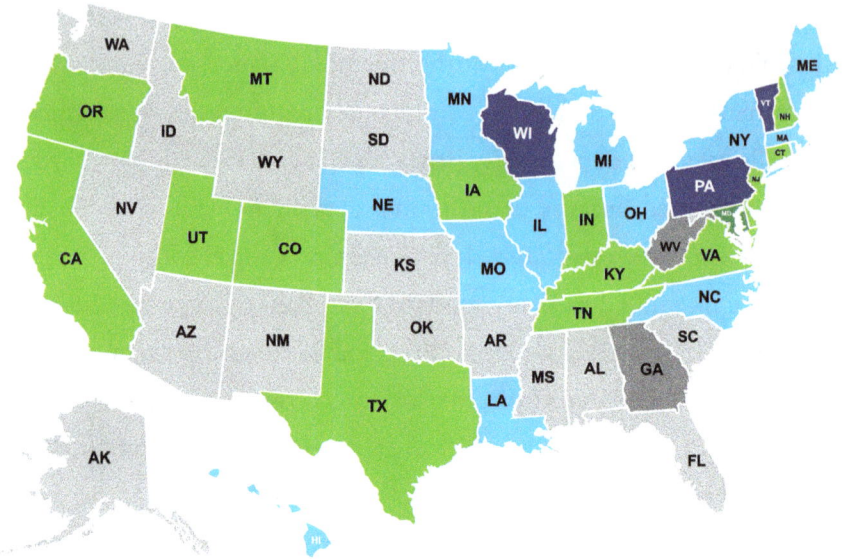

STATUTE/BILL IN LEGISLATIVE PROCESS

- Introduced
- In committee
- In cross chamber
- In cross committee
- Passed
- Signed
- Inactive bills
- No comprehensive bills introduced

Graphic courtesy of the International Association of Privacy Professionals
(Current as of May 2024)

How Will These New Compliance Risks Affect Your Life Sciences Business?

For decades, and now more than ever, having a chief compliance and/or chief privacy officer is critical. Though privacy and data security are different, they go together, and together they're giving rise to a new set of considerations. Commercial and business teams and senior leadership will need to adjust trainings, policies, and procedures. They should audit and monitor everything that goes along with ensuring strategies that are effective and enable responsible corporate citizenship.

But it is important to pause here for a moment. Yes, we are making progress in AI (discussed later) and the sheer amount of data accumulated. Here are some startling facts:

- A total of 90 percent of all the world's data has been created in the last two years. And the volume of the world's data is now doubling every two years.[27]

- The world generates **2.5 quintillion bytes** of data per day.[28]

That is an astounding amount, beyond the comprehension of most of us. Importantly, that data, *our* data needs to be protected and safe; our privacy is paramount. But let's not get our heads too wrapped up in quintillions and zettabytes (yes, that's an amount of data!). In the end, like all of compliance, there is a legal component, but it still comes down to people.

Every organization must have a set of core principles centered around protecting sensitive personal information with the utmost regard. It's about keeping the trust of your customers, the people whom you serve, and the people who work for you. Ultimately, senior leaders should ask themselves, "How would I want my family's healthcare information to be treated?"

The clear answer should be "With the utmost of care."

These kinds of questions can be powerful. Remember, when you humanize compliance, people connect doing the *right* thing with being the only path forward. This is how you inspire integrity, win with compliance, and propel performance!

---

27 Kevin Bartley, "Data Statistics (2024) - How Much Data Is There in the World?," Rivery, August 27, 2023, https://rivery.io/blog/big-data-statistics-how-much-data-is-there-in-the-world/.

28 Ibid.

Building a Culture of Compliance

An inspired approach from leadership builds a culture of compliance, meaning doing that right thing. It also builds integrity, loyalty, and security within your company culture, which, yes, yields added sales. Remember, this is what compliance is all about:

- Enhancing your credibility and reputation

- Building *trust*

- Insulating yourself against potential claims

There's a rational element here, but also a personal one that touches people's hearts because it makes abundant sense and has a measurable, net-positive business effect. For example, one silver lining that came out of the COVID-19 pandemic is faster-than-ever medical advancements. We are on the brink—in all sorts of research on diseases, from cancer to rare genetic disorders—of understanding what could lead to incredible scientific discoveries, but the side effects include drastically increased compliance risks.

Defining New Challenges

Enlightened leaders will define these new challenges as an opportunity to invest in and strengthen their organizations' privacy and data security processes. Be smart and build *trust* by investing in cutting-edge software that enhances your data security and privacy protections and that is thoughtfully applied by experts who understand your life sciences business and its unique mix of compliance and privacy risks.

One of the best ways to get started is to join the International Association of Privacy Professionals (IAPP), a resource for professionals who want to develop and implement ways to manage these privacy and data security risks. Let's face it, data greatly influences the information economy and the world, and the associated risks continue to rise, which include the following:

- Data breach

- Identity theft

- Loss of trust by consumers

- Financial losses from fines and lost business

- *Reputational loss*

In today's marketplace, these are threats that affect companies of all sizes. The IAPP is the world's most comprehensive and largest global information privacy community. It offers a variety of management practices and tools that help companies thrive in this rapidly changing information economy and the world. Building a company that does what's right, not just what's required, extends to privacy and data security as well.

Also keep in mind that it is much easier—as with all compliance programs—to deal with issues of data privacy before your company grows through mergers and acquisitions or other events that suddenly create a data crisis you are unprepared for.

Privacy and Security Are *Not* the Same Thing

As technology grows more complex and invasive, so does the use of the data. That scenario leaves organizations and companies at a huge risk for personal information being exposed. To be clear as to the difference between the two, *privacy* of data is focused on the use and control of personal data, such as putting policies in place that ensure personal information is being collected and used in suitable ways. On the other hand, *security* focuses on protecting that personal information and data from malicious attacks so that data is not exploited and misused. While security is an important consideration for protecting data, it is not sufficient for addressing privacy.

Companies and organizations that do not address privacy in their compliance program are at risk for the following:

- Class action lawsuits

- Government enforcement

- Financial ruin

- Damaged reputation

- Loss of customer loyalty

In today's world the issues and risks of privacy have become the new norm and a necessity for doing business. When it comes to a compliance program, you need to make sure that privacy issues are addressed correctly in your organization or company. It is important to thoroughly understand privacy and build the skills required and information needed to set up a successful compliance program that addresses these issues. Data privacy concerns in the pharmaceutical and life sciences industry are especially significant because of the sensitive nature of the data handled. The compliance concerns you need to be certain you are addressing include the following:

Patient Confidentiality and Sensitive Personal Data: Pharmaceuticals and life sciences companies handle highly sensitive personal data, including medical histories, genetic information, and other health-related data.

Your Organization's Legal and Ethical Obligations: Ensuring the confidentiality of this data is not only a legal obligation under laws such as HIPAA in the United States and GDPR in the EU but also an ethical responsibility.

Cybersecurity Threats: The industry is a target for cyberattacks because of the value of the data. Breaches can lead to unauthorized access to sensitive patient information.

Data Encryption and Access Controls: Implementing robust encryption methods and strict access controls is crucial to protect data from unauthorized access.

Global Regulations: Compliance with various global data protection regulations is complex. Different regions have different laws (e.g., GDPR, CCPA, HIPAA), and companies must ensure they meet all applicable requirements.

Consent Management: Obtaining and managing patient consent for data usage is critical to comply with regulations and respect patient autonomy.

Accuracy and Reliability: Ensuring the accuracy and reliability of data is essential for research and development, as well as for maintaining patient safety.

Data Governance: Establishing strong data governance frameworks helps maintain data integrity and quality throughout its life cycle.

Vendor and Third-Party Management: Engaging with third-party vendors for data processing or storage introduces additional risks. Ensuring these vendors comply with data protection standards is vital.

Data Sharing and Collaboration: Collaborations with external researchers, partners, or institutions require careful management of data sharing agreements to safeguard privacy.

Clinical Trials: Handling data from clinical trials involves managing large volumes of sensitive information. Ensuring anonymization and secure handling is crucial.

Intellectual Property: Protecting intellectual property while maintaining data privacy is a delicate balance, especially in collaborative research efforts.

Big Data and AI: The use of big data and AI in research and personalized medicine brings additional privacy concerns. Ensuring data is anonymized and securely handled is crucial.

Internet of Things and Wearables: Devices that collect health data must be designed with privacy in mind, ensuring secure data transmission and storage.

Addressing these data privacy concerns requires a comprehensive approach that includes strong technical measures, regulatory compliance, effective data governance, and a commitment to ethical standards in handling sensitive information.

If data privacy is important, if compliance is important, then there must be those with their ears to the ground, anticipating issues before they become crises. Imperative to that sort of oversight is the role of the board of directors, which we will discuss in the next chapter.

CHAPTER 6:

THE IMPORTANCE OF ACTIVE BOARD OVERSIGHT

If you think compliance is expensive, try non-compliance.

—PAUL MCNULTY, FORMER DEPUTY U.S. ATTORNEY GENERAL

A ctive board oversight in the pharmaceutical industry is a critical component for ensuring corporate governance, regulatory compliance, and strategic alignment. In a sector characterized by rapid innovation, complex regulatory landscapes, and significant ethical considerations, the role of the board extends beyond traditional fiduciary responsibilities. Remember the mother of the child with a rare, deadly disease. This goes far beyond boardrooms, conference tables, and annual reports. An active board can help prevent the sorts of disasters that can derail bringing a powerful new drug to market or destroy a company entirely through negligence or a lack of oversight.

Instead, effective oversight by the board of directors involves a deep understanding of the unique challenges and opportunities within the pharmaceutical industry, including the development and commercialization of new drugs, management of clinical trials, and navigation of global regulatory frameworks. Active board oversight ensures that companies adhere to stringent safety and ethical standards, maintain transparency in their operations, and align their strategies with long-term sustainability and shareholder value. It also involves rigorous scrutiny of risk management practices, particularly in areas such as drug safety, patent protection, and market competition. By fostering a culture of integrity, accountability, and ethical behavior, the board can mitigate risks associated with legal and regulatory noncompliance, financial mismanagement, and reputational damage. Moreover, the board's proactive engagement in strategic decision-making processes, such as mergers and acquisitions, R&D investments, and market expansion, is essential for driving innovation and maintaining competitive advantage.

As the pharmaceutical landscape evolves with advancements in biotechnology, personalized medicine, and digital health, the need for knowledgeable and proactive board oversight becomes even more pronounced. This chapter explores the multifaceted role of board oversight in the pharmaceutical industry, highlighting best practices, challenges, and the impact of effective governance on corporate success and industry advancement. Additionally, investors who are on the board of directors help fund the company, whether it is privately or publicly held or looking to go public. *Financial and fiduciary oversight is not just a part of compliance; it is essential.*

Regardless of your company's financial situation, it's critical to get your compliance program in shape, especially when working with a major bank, because banks will evaluate your compliance programs to assess and minimize their risk. To know whether your compliance program passes the test, ask the following key questions:

1. Are you protecting investors' funding to address key risks?

2. Do you have the right people leading your program?

3. Is the company and your program structured the right way?

It is not enough to simply have a compliance program serve as a *de facto* insurance policy. In fact, major financial institutions are now insisting that companies they work with have credible, functioning compliance programs that pass muster. A good compliance program operates in accordance with applicable laws and regulations. It creates a culture of honesty and integrity while meeting high ethical and professional standards. A good compliance program prevents fraud and abuse and becomes a nonnegotiable element of organizational strategy. It needs to be well designed, applied earnestly and in good faith, adequately resourced, and empowered to function effectively—and it must work in the "real" world.

Mistakes to Avoid

One of the biggest mistakes that companies make is not involving the board of directors early enough and sufficiently in the design and oversight of the compliance program. It's understandable perhaps that executives may feel like they don't want to bother the board with nitty-gritty risk issues, but that can be a serious mistake when it comes to effective compliance. Remember the landmark case I cited earlier in the book, *In re Caremark International Inc.*, which was decided in 1996 by the Delaware Court of Chancery? It was all about board oversight.[29]

In that case the court decided that individual board members, and the board as a whole, were liable for the compliance failures of the company. Why? Because the board did not exercise active oversight of the company compliance program—and that, in turn, breached

---

29   Jim DeLoach, "Caremark: Even the Highest Standards Can Be Met," December 23, 2020, https://www.corporatecomplianceinsights.com/caremark-highest-standard-boards/.

their fiduciary duties to the company. It raised the question regarding compliance, asking, "What is the board's responsibility with respect to the organization and monitoring of the enterprise to assure that the corporation functions within the law to achieve its purposes?"

The shareholders of Caremark International, Inc. alleged that the directors breached their duty of care by failing to put in place adequate internal control systems. This, in turn, enabled the company's employees to commit criminal offenses that resulted in substantial fines and civil penalties totaling more than $250 million.

The settlement required stricter oversight of corporate employees, and the board of directors was authorized to approve or reject significant transactions, capital structure, and even compensation of the CEO. It was also determined that a corporate information and reporting system must exist, and failure to do so, under certain circumstances, would render a director liable for losses.

Defining Active Board Oversight

So what does active board oversight look like? It involves regular briefings and meetings with the board, which generally means quarterly compliance reports for larger, more complex corporations and semiannually for smaller ones. More specifically, in the earlier stages of compliance program development for a company, that means reporting the findings of a risk assessment, for example, and recommendations on how to address the results of that assessment. It also means submitting various documents to the board for review and approval, including core compliance documents, such as the company code of business conduct, and a company compliance charter. Each of these interactions, of course, should be fully documented to form an ongoing record to evidence the board's active involvement. Failure to do this exposes the company, and specifically the board, to potential liability in the event of any compliance failure.

Just as importantly, as an internal matter, active board involvement in the design, implementation, and oversight of the compliance program signals to executives and employees the relative priority and importance of the compliance program to the company. In other words it helps establish the tone at the top with the commensurate credibility to inspire and motivate everyone in the company to adopt a culture of integrity, which will yield compliance as an outcome. This type of active board oversight in the design, development, and implementation of a compliance program has been at best inconsistent among different companies in the past. This is why, in part, current OIG CIAs spell out specific board obligations and certification requirements to ensure a board's active involvement in compliance oversight as a mandatory part of the CIA.

It's far better to have active board oversight before anything like a CIA is imposed upon a company.

Financial Implications

I would also suggest there are indeed financial incentives for boards to take the time and make the effort to be actively involved and oversee the compliance program. Here is why: a properly implemented compliance program can add value to the company. Conversely, an insufficient or ineffective program can reduce or diminish its value, especially if there are compliance failures as a result. In any M&A transaction, a company acquires the compliance failures of the company it buys. So it behooves the acquiring company to do thorough due diligence of the target company's compliance program. I've lived through both sides of these types of M&A transactions, both as the target company being purchased and as an acquiring company looking to buy a target. The due diligence needs to be comprehensive, scouring every available document to review the compliance program for its structure and consistency in meeting the Seven Elements. I have also served as a compliance expert for a company under a CIA, where the nature and level of review are similar. You need to assess the effectiveness of the program relative to the DOJ guidance referenced earlier. In short, you need to answer the following three questions:

1. Is the corporation's compliance program well designed?

2. Is the program being applied earnestly and in good faith? In other words is the program adequately resourced and empowered to function effectively?

3. Does the corporation's compliance program work in practice?[30]

The following areas are to be considered when it comes to active board involvement.

EFFECTIVE LEADERSHIP

Returning to the overall theme woven throughout this book, I want to underscore the importance of effective board leadership. Active board involvement signals to executives and the entire company that if the board is involved, it *must* be important and a priority. An active board is critically important for setting the right tone and culture and setting up the company for success in integrating compliance into its operational DNA. Again, this is about inspiring integrity and defining success so that everyone equates compliance with executing the mission of the company successfully and with integrity. The mission is what is critical (e.g., finding a cure or providing a lifesaving therapy for a rare form of

---

30 US Department of Justice Criminal Division, "Evaluation of Corporate Compliance Programs," updated March 2023, 1–2.

pediatric cancer), and this should inspire everyone to work with integrity and not jeopardize that inspirational goal with a compliance failure.

RELUCTANT BOARD CHALLENGE

A challenge for any compliance officer is encountering a reluctant board that doesn't want to get involved with any of these matters. In the past some boards only reluctantly made time on their packed board agenda for compliance training. Why? They rightly feared, perhaps, that the training would waste their time, be boring, and irrelevant to their level of risks. This is why compliance officers need to seize the moment when in front of the board to make the best impression and keep the information presented relevant, interesting, and memorable. Your goal should be to make them realize that compliance is an opportunity that provides value and mitigates risk. This is where transformational leadership, vision, and involving the concepts of ethics and integrity can help inspire. The board needs to buy into compliance as an integral part of the mission—the board needs to be inspired too!

CODES OF CONDUCT

Most board executives are seasoned professionals, intelligent former CEOs, current CEOs, or retired executives, and they don't like wasting their time. Identify with precision the issues that they are most likely to encounter from a compliance perspective. Conflicts of interest are the most common issue, followed by privacy and data security issues. Regardless of their area of expertise, everyone can relate to the modern complications of technology risks.

When it comes to conflicts of interest, board members tend to have incredible networks; they are often asked to refer people for employment, business opportunities for sponsorship, charitable causes, or references. Not all conflicts are bad, but the key is to disclose all information up front and allow the company board of directors to make an appropriate determination regarding conflict. As a compliance professional, you need to understand what to present, how to present it, and focus on key takeaway issues. For example, this would include planning, implementing, and overseeing risk-related programs and creating and coordinating proper reporting channels for compliance issues. Developing company compliance communications, coordinating, and scheduling required compliance training for employees should also be presented.

Here's another piece of advice I have learned from experience: Board members do not like being preached to—for any reason! However, most *are* open to learning. Finding the delicate balance between communication forms means identifying likely areas of interest for your audience. One excellent approach is to provide cases and scenarios where the answers are not clear cut and where perhaps you list pros and cons. If you then provide clear guidance and outcomes, you're likely to find that board will come to respect your information, compliance at large, and (perhaps most importantly from your perspective) ... *you*!

QUANTITATIVELY ORIENTED

Most boards and board members are quantitatively oriented, meaning they like objective data. To a degree, you can present relevant data in terms of the compliance program and performance through a comprehensive dashboard that shows progress against a specific work plan, such as a percentage of completions, training, or any type of misconduct. This means showing data that the compliance program is working effectively and is backed up with data and facts. The figures here offer an example. For a busy board of directors who may not have a background in compliance, it speaks in "board language"—clear, concise, facts.

Sample Compliance Dashboard

Status of U.S Compliance Program Implementation by Program Element ("7 Elements") + U.S. Privacy Program & Compliance Risk Assessment Findings

1: Implement Written Standards	2: Designate a Compliance Officer and Compliance Committee	3: Conduct Effective Training & Education
4: Develop Effective Lines of Communication	5: Enforce Standards through Well-Publicized Disciplinary Guidelines	6: Conduct Internal Monitoring and Auditing
7: Respond Promptly to Detected Offenses and Undertake Corrective Action	U.S. Privacy Program [*Budget approved; contract awaiting signatures.]	Addressing Compliance Risk Assessment Findings

Overall Progress Towards Program Elements

Status Key
- Complete
- On track
- At risk
- Past due
- Under Development

U.S. Compliance Program Resource Statistics FY'25

Personnel	FTEs		Outsourced Headcount	
Personnel	0		1	

Financials	FY'24-'25 Budget	FY'25-'27 Budget Items Under review & recommended	Current Total FY'25-26 Budget Forecast	Spend to Date since 01/01/25	Status
	$200,000 (USD) + Hotline costs ($1,500.)	• $400,000 24-Month Contract Extension • US Privacy Program Support $100,000.00 • FMV Support $12-$15K (FMV Support) • Hotline ($1,500.00 Annual Fee on 2-year contract with Vendor X.)	$350k (USD)	$200,000 (USD)	G — 12-month Contract extension and U.S. Privacy Program Support contract submitted for signature

U.S. Commercial Compliance Executive Summary

- Overall, implementation of the U.S. Commercial Compliance Program is on track.
  1. Compliance Monitoring Implemented
  2. Compliance Audit completed
  3. Code of Conduct and policies and business rules reviewed for 2025
  4. Code of Conduct Compliance training nearly complete (See statistics on next slide)
  5. Conducted targeted Compliance training for sales force and MSL teams (See next slide)
  6. Successfully conferred with Law Firm X re: FDA assistance
  7. Rigorous LMR review and approval of marketing and medical materials content and purpose is ongoing
  8. Requisite state reporting and state registrations completed on time
  9. 2025 US Federal Open Payments report submitted on time
  10. Prep for 2026 US Federal Open Payments Reporting process in process with external vendors and internal team
  11. Compliance Committee meeting is scheduled for Nov. 1st

- Open Items:
  1. Address U.S. Privacy compliance risks (Q4'25)
  2. Certify on company website Compliance Program Meets CA requirements (7 elements) (Certification language submitted.)
  3. Consider employing more rigorous FMV methodology
  4. Ensure all employees complete required Code of Conduct Training for 2025 (Q4) (See next Slide)

TRESTLE

PROTECTED BY THE ATTORNEY-CLIENT PRIVILEGE AND WORK-PRODUCT DOCTRINE

Sample Compliance Dashboard (cont'd)

2025 Code of Conduct Annual Compliance Training
Status of Completion

Division	Completion Status
US	39/47 (83%)
Canada	62/75 (83%)
Europe	3/5*(60%)
	* (Likely to be reduced to 0)
Board of Directors	8/8* (100%)
	*(Assumes completion by members not at live/virtual session to be via pre-recorded video session)
Total	112/135 (83%)

[Please Note: Follow-up in progress for 100% completion by Q4.]

Code of Conduct and Targeted Compliance Training Conducted Q4'25- 2026

1. In-office meals & Proper Communications Refresher – Dec. 12, 2025
2. POA Kick-off: Compliance Refresher – Feb 08, 2026
3. Transparency Reporting Update -- May 10, 2026
4. Annual Code of Conduct Training –
   - All Employees: June 10, 2026 & Sept. 25, 2026 (make-up)
   - Board: Aug. 15, 2026

Compliance Questions/ Hotline Calls

- Number of Hotline Calls: 4
- Number of Direct Calls from Field Sales, Marketing, Medical: 12
- Number of emails re: Compliance Questions/Support from Field: 120+
  - Topics Addressed:
    1. Speaker programs: Topics. Presentations, Venues, Review, Approval
    2. Commercial and Medical Interactions, Coordination, Separation
    3. State Reporting
    4. Transparency Reporting
    5. Discussion about Sunshine reporting for symposium attendees and vetting of menu / meal costs
    6. POA
    7. NJ Meal Caps
- Number of calls with Legal Team: 1-2/week
- LMR (Legal Medical Review) Committee Calls: 1/week

Field Monitoring Conducted 2025-'26

- Speaker Program, NYC, Nov. 11, 2025
- Speaker Program, Houston, TX, Nov. 20, 2025
- MSL Program, Feb. 14, 2026, Orlando, Fl,
- Field Sales Ride Along, Oct. 12, 2026

TRESTLE

PROTECTED BY THE ATTORNEY-CLIENT PRIVILEGE AND WORK-PRODUCT DOCTRINE

Sample of data-driven compliance dashboard

When you show a level of completion, you are providing assurance and peace of mind to the board by showing your comprehensive and thorough command of the compliance requirements. They are looking to you to be the compliance leader to provide assurance that the company is moving in the right direction.

As the world's regulators penalize companies with increasingly steep fines for corporate misconduct, compliance officers are becoming critical linchpins to protect the company, stop executives from going to jail, and prevent unethical conduct. However, with greater visibility comes the need for a greater skill set. It's clear that the most effective people in the compliance profession have shifted from the mentality of merely being a qualified compliance professional into one who is seen as an executive leader and an asset to the business. It is no longer enough (I would suggest it never was) to simply "check the boxes of compliance" and be adequate. Instead, businesses need super effective compliance officers who can persuade and motivate the business to do the right thing and to be truly *emotionally* invested in the aims of the compliance program, which is to inspire integrity by tying compliance to the larger mission and purpose of the company.

At the same time, when and if necessary, coordinated with the executive team, you can share candid recommendations and/or areas of risk for the company. In other words you don't want to be just a "yes-person" with nothing but good news; you have to share needs and challenges, as well as accomplishments. This is a delicate matter because being a compliance officer often requires careful coordination with the executive team. What you don't want to do is appear like you are going over their head and dropping a bomb in a board meeting that may be unnecessary and cause undue alarm. That is something that can get any inexperienced compliance officer fired—and frankly, rightly so.

For example, in the life sciences industry, maintaining compliance requires a high degree of preparation for the digital future, and that includes highly responsive cybersecurity strategies that can protect against revolving threats. Hackers continue to become more advanced at launching attacks on unsuspecting personnel and often use social media to get sensitive business details that can be used for phishing attacks. Each attack has the potential to bring ruin to a life sciences organization through lost revenue, reduced customer trust, and the costs associated with remediation and communication efforts. Privacy, as we established in the last chapter, is the new compliance.

You need to use good judgment because there is so much on the line with compliance regulations. Anything presented to the board or in a meeting can be subpoenaed. This is also why you want to keep the written words on the page to a minimum by using bullet points in your presentation so you can speak more generally that allow for a better flow of ideas. Using bullet points allows you to address the challenge or delicate matter without writing out all the details. Plus, it can keep you organized and on time (very important with any board!).

Attorney-Client Privilege

Chief compliance officers must work closely with the chief legal officer or GC on several important issues. In certain circumstances chief compliance officers must be mindful of the importance of the company's ability to assert the attorney–client privilege. While chief compliance officers tend to lean in favor of disclosure and transparency as an important principle in promoting a company's compliance program, there are several situations when compliance requires protection of the attorney–client privilege.

Lawyers and compliance officers need to pay close attention to the attorney–client privilege and make sure they take proper steps to protect and promote the use of privilege in appropriate circumstances. When conducting serious internal investigations or reviewing significant compliance issues, a company's ability to cloak such determinations with the privilege is critical to the review, the company's decision, and the remediation of the issue, if warranted.

To review the basics, the attorney–client privilege applies to the following:

- Communications between an individual and an attorney (or someone acting at the direction of an attorney).

- Communications between a compliance officer and an in-house counsel can qualify for the attorney–client privilege so long as it is intended to seek, obtain, or provide legal guidance or services.

Compliance officers frequently consult in-house attorneys for guidance on the law, development of compliance policies, and day-to-day discussion of legal implications of compliance issues. A compliance officer may use legal advice from in-house counsel to provide guidance and respond to an employee question, enforce the company's compliance policies and procedures, conduct investigations, take corrective actions, and provide reports to corporate leaders to address specific situations for your company. Chances are, you will want to have the option to share all the work that you have done, including the following:

- Risk assessments

- Investigations

- Corrective actions taken

It is about maintaining control of the information so that in the event you are asked for something, you can gather that information to present to those who need it. Without the attorney–client privilege, you would be forced to present this without full context, and you, as the compliance officer, do not want to appear like you are hiding something. Engage in open and thoughtful conversations on a legal matter so you can develop an appropriate and legal approach to any issue that needs to be addressed.

Now that we have spent a good portion of the book discussing the land mines of compliance and how important it is to have ears to the ground, written policies in place, and people who understand that life and death can be on the line in compliance in the life sciences, it's time to look at a five-step process you can utilize to create an effective commercial compliance program.

CHAPTER 7:

APPLYING THEORY TO PRACTICE: THE FIVE-STEP PROCESS TO CREATING EFFECTIVE COMMERCIAL COMPLIANCE

n this chapter we are going to apply compliance solutions that add real-world value through a five-step process. This is a framework you can adapt to your company (even better if you have a compliance sherpa who uses this system). Let me offer an example. You may be a CEO, board member, or private equity investor of a specialty pharmaceutical/biotech company focused on rare diseases with products in phase III clinical trials. If so, then to date, you have undoubtedly been focused on the science and the next round of funding, as this is what will build your "baby," make your dreams come true, and enable you to live your passion in your biotech company.

You might be a physician, a PhD scientist, a former pharma executive, some combination of these, or all the above. No doubt, you have been utterly consumed, working feverishly and passionately to build your core team, attract top talent and investors, and meet research and funding milestones. All of this is done in a relentless effort to bring a breakthrough therapy to the market for the benefit of patients and their families, who are likely suffering from a rare disease with little, if any, other alternatives.

On the distant but fast-approaching horizon, you can see that moment when all this effort will bear fruit—the moment you receive FDA approval to launch your product. You are anywhere from eighteen, twelve, or even six months out from anticipated approval. You may even have won expedited review. Wow! This is the moment that you, your scientists, your team, your investors, and most importantly, your patients have been waiting for.

More than likely you have hired a GC, who, on the one hand, is likely experienced in intellectual property issues and general corporate matters but, on the other hand, may have only a smattering, if any, knowledge of the specific commercial compliance requirements to launch and commercialize a product. You appreciate that these commercial compliance requirements need to be addressed but don't want to do too much too soon because you need to keep things moving fast.

No doubt, you have either begun the search for or have hired a chief commercial officer to lead and develop the extensive launch plans and to build out the sales and marketing team. However, what you likely haven't done is hire a chief compliance officer. Yes, you know it's important, and you are fully supportive of having the appropriate and necessary compliance program in place, but at the right time. For now, it can wait. After all, the biggest risks and focus for federal and state regulatory enforcement authorities revolve around the sales, marketing, and pricing of FDA-approved products.

Co-pay patient assistance programs, HIPAA privacy, pricing, off-label marketing, antikickback concerns regarding physician interactions, false claims, and associated federal and state reporting requirements are the hot bread-and-butter compliance issues that arise in a commercial context today. As you are not there yet, you can put commercial compliance on the back burner. Right?

Funding is tight, as it always is, and let's face it, once you hire the compliance officer, the freedom, flexibility, speed, and nimbleness that you have enjoyed to date will be reduced and constrained by the requisite new policies, procedures, training, auditing, monitoring, etc. Right? Why impose those costs and constraints now? Technically, there is no law that requires it now, right? Why not wait until there is a more imminent need? Isn't timing everything?

Yes, timing is everything—but so is trust. Trust takes time to earn. The time to integrate and evolve your commercial compliance program is, in fact, *now*. If done properly, this is an opportunity to create an effective commercial culture that unleashes the maximum energy of your commercial team to compete and win confidently and, yes, compliantly. It's about integrating appropriate, scaled, measured, thoughtful compliance solutions into the DNA of commercial strategy, tactics, and execution. It's about creating a cohesive commercial compliance team that is built on a foundation of trust.

As with all human relationships, trust is built over time and comes from repeated interactions that demonstrate shared commitment, shared reliability, shared dependability, and shared success. Yes, it's about winning, but winning the *right* way, the ethical and compliant way. Launch time, or even a few weeks or months before launch, is certainly not when you want to start the trust-building process. If you want to do it right, start now.

The Right Strategy and Execution

Over the past two decades, much has been learned about how to best implement life science commercial compliance to be successful.

I have been honored to be part of some of these concepts and to be focused on welcoming changes that will make our industry better. Much like in the world of science and biotech, where the innermost workings of our DNA have come to be understood and mapped to develop custom therapies for patients and rare diseases, so, too, the commercial/compliance DNA has been unraveled, sequenced, and understood to produce a much more effective life science commercial compliance business model.

Both government regulators and private practitioners have a much more detailed understanding of the specific risks, timing, and scaling up of an effective commercial compliance program. What, in retrospect, was more of a meat cleaver approach to commercial compliance is now much more surgically precise and, as a result, both more cost-effective and operationally effective.

As with any major initiative, it is important to take a moment to step back and thoughtfully assess the big picture. Start with the end in mind and identify key drivers and factors that pertain to your unique set of circumstances. Define what success looks like from a commercial/compliance perspective. Then gain consensus around this definition and develop a joint commercial/compliance strategy that integrates commercial goals and timing within an agreed-upon compliance structure.

Sequence, roll out, and scale up your commercial operations in unison with carefully coordinated compliance processes and compliance structural elements in an efficient, effective effort. Explore new solutions to meet unique challenges by identifying and applying key core principles. Here are some key questions to start with:

- How do we best engage patients, physicians, and providers without running afoul of compliance issues? Prelaunch? Postlaunch?

- How do we appropriately balance the appearance and reality of high prices with patient benefits with co-pay assistance programs?

- How do we best communicate publicly both the benefits and the risks of our product in any SEC-regulated disclosure?

Identify specific tactics to execute the strategy effectively and consistently. Then ... execute, execute, execute while measuring continuously, adjusting as needed, and reporting and communicating results. This can only be done well by commercial and compliance colleagues who trust and respect each other, who, with sleeves rolled up, tackle each challenge *with shared commitment and passion to achieve a common, clearly defined, shared goal.*

Don't wait to put your chief compliance officer and commercial compliance program in place. Start now to build that foundation of trust, and you will experience a successful launch that will meet your commercial goals and your compliance requirements. Most importantly, you will build a solid foundation for a company culture built on trust that will position you for many successful launches in the future and will win the respect of your employees.

By doing so, you will also earn the trust of patients, investors, shareholders, and government regulators while increasing your company's reputational capital and reducing your risk to whistleblowers and enforcement actions. Truly a win-win-win outcome across the board. The time to build trust is always now.

In the following sections, we will cover my Five-Step Process for Commercial/Compliance Success, which is as follows:

FIVE-STEP PROCESS FOR COMMERCIAL/ COMPLIANCE SUCCESS

Step 1: Define Success and Gain Consensus. What do they look like for you?

Step 2: Develop a Shared Commercial/Compliance Implementation Strategy

Step 3: Map Out a Detailed Shared Execution Plan

Step 4: Execute Your Plan Collaboratively

Step 5: Measure and Report Your Results

Step 1: Define Success and Gain Consensus. What Do They Look Like for You?

Quality is never an accident; it is always the result of high intention, sincere effort, intelligent direction and skillful execution; it represents the wise choice of many alternatives.

—WILLIAM A. FOSTER

As every leader knows, the key to inspiring and motivating a team is to define their goal and mission or what success looks like for them. Think of just about every underdog sports movie ever made—*Rudy, A League of Their Own, Remember the Titans* ... The coach inevitably comes into the locker room at halftime and inspires the team to come together—and win!

What is your team's raison d'être, or justification for existence? Once defined, strong leaders can laser focus and develop the tactics to achieve their goal and mission. As a life sciences CEO, board member, or investor, you're motivated to change the lives of patients. For patients who may be suffering from a rare disease and may have no other options, *this is the magic of life sciences and biotech industries—the ability to discover new therapies and find solutions for people who have not had them in the past*—and that takes a lot of money, time, and risk.

You have gone through the research and development phase, the science, therapies, modules, and development portion, and now it is time to get approval. Once approved for commercialization, the last thing you want is for your team to blow up the opportunity that you have worked so hard for years to create. How would they blow this up? By inadvertently or, candidly, stupidly taking unnecessary compliance risks in selling and marketing your product.

SALES AND MARKETING ARE YOUR HIGHEST COMPLIANCE RISKS

Every major settlement in the life sciences industry to date has involved inappropriate sales and marketing activities. To say that sales and marketing are your highest compliance risks is a statement of the obvious. Here's why: when you look at the biggest pharma lawsuits by settlement amounts, they all have an explanation of similarities.

Take TAP Pharmaceuticals, for example, which paid approximately $875 million for fraudulent drug pricing and marketing practices for its prostate cancer drug, Lupron. The settlement amount included $290 million for a criminal fee, $559.4 million for filing false and misleading claims with the Medicare and Medicaid programs, and $25.5 million for filing false and misleading claims within all states of the United States in 2000. The company offered various incentives to healthcare providers and other customers, such as the following:

- Free drugs and medications

- Trips to resorts

- Medical equipment

- Consultation services for prescribing Lupron to the beneficiaries of Medicare program

In a horrifying nutshell, TAP violated the Prescription Drug Marketing Act and charged several elderly beneficiaries of the Medicare program, as well as the program directly, for free samples of Lupron. TAP Pharmaceuticals was formed as a joint venture between two worldwide pharmaceutical companies, Abbott Laboratories and Takeda Pharmaceutical Company, in 1977. The two companies agreed to dissolve the joint venture in 2008. Their most lucrative products included a proton-pump inhibitor known as Prevacid and Lupron. The purpose of the joint venture was to get products that Takeda had discovered, approved, and marketed in the United States and Canada.

When the settlement was announced, the DOJ also proclaimed that seven people were indicted on criminal charges by a grand jury. Four doctors pled guilty to receiving kickbacks; twelve TAP employees were indicted and contested the charges. However, in July 2004, a federal jury in Boston declared all the defendants not guilty. Abbott kept the rights to Lupron, which had sales of over $600 million in 2007, with a patent expiring in 2015, while Takeda kept the rights to lansoprazole (Prevacid), which had sales of $2.3 billion in 2007, but both agreed to end the partnership in 2008. Takeda was obligated to pay Abbott about $1.5 billion over several years. By 2008, Takeda's sales outside of TAP had grown to $3 billion, mostly from the best-selling drug for diabetes in the world.

What does all this mean for you? You need to address sales and marketing (and the compliance related to it) with the same vigor, energy, and passion that you addressed the science and financing that got you to this stage. Any settlement that involves off-label marketing, false claims, or kickbacks is directly related to inappropriate sales and marketing (in other words, commercial activity). The top ten settlements alone total over $5 billion over twenty years. As the late Senator Everett Dirksen said, "A billion here or a billion there, and pretty soon you're talking about real money." Real money, indeed.

INTEGRATE COMPLIANCE INTO YOUR COMPANY'S DNA

For companies preparing to pivot from a research and development organization to a commercial one, it is imperative that you integrate a culture of compliance into the DNA of your commercial organization. As the leader, you are not beholden to any kind of democratic process when it comes to defining your company and its goals. This is your company and your vision—your baby. You have been successful in identifying unique science to bring about distinctive therapies and solutions with the funding to demonstrate their efficacy.

How do you bring that to market? Selling your product in the marketplace with appropriate boundaries is critically important. Again, it is about doing what is right, not just what is required. As the leader, you are the most important person who sets the "tone at the top" that will guide everyone else in your organization. That is why, above all else, you need to develop a core set of principles and values that will guide all behavior in your company. It is from these core values and principles that the concept of compliance and, more specifically, ethics and compliance will flow.

Remember, people and teams are not inspired and motivated by rules and requirements, but they *are* inspired and motivated by principles and values that lead to accomplishing life-changing goals, something that is truly special. Principles and values do not need to be long and boring; they can be short, crisp, relevant, and memorable. This is why Inspiring Integrity is How You Win with Compliance and Propel Performance. It works!

JOHNSON & JOHNSON

Perhaps the most famous company in this area of compliance is Johnson & Johnson. They stand by their credo, and it features prominently on their website and in their corporate information. The code of ethics and compliance dates to 1943, when Robert Wood Johnson himself crafted it. Johnson & Johnson was founded to help meet safer medical needs and sterile surgical products that could help save lives while making doctors' jobs easier. This blend of concern for the health of humanity and business savvy continues to characterize the company throughout its history, now, and for years to come.

Historically, most companies have not done what Johnson & Johnson did in terms of compliance. However, today, more and more start-up companies are implementing a compliance program. Thirty years ago, it was not thought of as a separate function but simply integrated into the law department, and the lawyers determined whether something was legal or not. In terms of the life sciences industry, ethics and compliance programs have only been around since the early 2000s, with the TAP case and Pfizer leading the way.

Up to that point, the credo of Johnson & Johnson was focused on principle-oriented guideposts for their corporate behavior. Other than that, most companies approached compliance as a very legalistic dos and don'ts process, and that is why it failed. It did not inspire or motivate people other than to go through the training and avoid getting into trouble. The compliance program was never envisioned as an organization that provided solutions and empowered the sales force to compete and win. The corporate handcuffs were driven by lawyers, and that turned people off. They went through the training program checking off the boxes, but compliance was not woven into the corporate DNA.

Ironically enough, I learned from the sales force how to connect with people and build relationships and applied those lessons internally to connect with employees and inspire them to comply with appropriate boundaries. Again, compliance leaders must explain the why behind the what in a sincere and credible effort to prevent misconduct and not just be seen as enforcers lowering the boom on violators.

The heavy-handed corporate cop approach to compliance simply scares people, which causes many to either keep their heads down and not volunteer any information or to simply leave and find employment elsewhere. The net result to the company as a whole is ironically greater risk. Why? The culture of fear that ensues pushes perceived compliance concerns outward and not inward. This allows these problems to grow hidden from view and spawns whistleblowers who go outside the company to address them and not inside to solve them. Remember, historically, the statistics overwhelmingly show that the greatest risk to any company is from an internal whistleblower. Every major settlement had a whistleblower. The culture of fear doesn't work.

The way to avoid a compliance program being perceived as becoming nothing but a litany of rules and regulations that threaten penalties for violations is, again, to lead with principles and values—it's back to inspiring integrity. That is how you define success and inspire and motivate a team while reaching a consensus to achieve your goals. From a CEO's perspective, there is enough to deal with from the board of directors; adding the sales and marketing team, research, and all that is involved with running the business all at the same time can be and has been overwhelming for some.

Your compliance officer should become your trusted advisor, advising you and your team on compliance boundaries, identifying areas that are black and white and where some may be gray, and explaining why!

CASE STUDY: THE ST. PAUL OF COMPLIANCE

For example, here is a case study (based on my real experiences) of a bright, intelligent entrepreneur—a CEO who graduated from the Wharton School of Business. This person was successful in creating value and reacted effectively to the concept of a corporate compliance officer and inquired on his first day on the job about his company's compliance processes or program. When I had first been hired as a compliance officer, it was for the largest publicly traded medical billing company that followed the Columbia HCA model—it focused on the bottom line and acquired the most successful medical billing companies across the country and loosely tied them together under a larger corporate umbrella. This flurry of M&A activity bought mostly mom-and-pop medical billing companies that had very independent entrepreneurs running each business. They were scooped up and left to run as independently as possible, only loosely tied to the corporation. However, because of the loose corporate structure, there was no central, shared compliance program in place, and sure enough, that led to a federal subpoena and a federal investigation.

I was then recruited to create the very first compliance program for the entire corporation. Since I was just learning what was in place, I called the attorney of one of these companies and left a message. That same day I received a phone call from the CEO, who was yelling at me at the top of his lungs.

I had to hold the phone at arm's length as he screamed with four-letter words, "How dare you call my company without asking me first to question my policies and procedures?" He went on to say, "I run a tight ship. If you have a question, you have to go through me."

After I got my hearing back, I politely tried to calm the gentleman down and said, "I certainly did not mean to be offensive to you or anyone else. My intent was to contact a relative peer of mine to get some information in a very constructive way."

Well, that began our working relationship, and the good news is that this gentleman, who was vehemently opposed to any inquiry into his business, became the strongest, most passionate advocate for compliance. In fact, I would call him the St. Paul of Compliance. Once he saw "the light," so to speak, he was the most passionate advocate of compliance. After conducting some research and interviews, I shared with him what I had found: that he had created a culture of fear. His employees feared him and were afraid to share their concerns. I told him that this was his number one compliance risk—you can't solve a problem you don't know about. I advised him that he needed to open up and speak with his employees and show his true self, that he genuinely wanted to fix problems that existed. His reaction was blunt disbelief. "Bullshit, Steve. My employees know that I am a man of integrity, that I am fair, and yes, that I am tough." Well, to his credit, he followed my advice and held an all-employee meeting, where he agreed to be open and honest with his employees and encouraged them to do the same. As a result he learned things he never imagined. To him and his employees' credit, they came forward and were very honest as to their fear to come forward with concerns, and he admitted he was a hard-ass CEO but shared in the desire to fix what was broken, all in a relentless goal to be the very best at what they do. In the end, everyone was unified and inspired by the call to openness and integrity in the pursuit of unparalleled excellence. I earned this leader's trust, and we had earned each other's respect. He was indeed a good man, a driven, passionate leader, with a bit of a gruff exterior. My experience with these types of leaders is, don't be intimidated by the gruff and tough exterior. Hold your ground as long as you can back up your position. These leaders will listen to you if you earn their respect. Don't be a CEO in denial. Instead, see the light of compliance and inspire integrity to win with compliance and propel performance, as this CEO did. *See the light from day one.*

Step 2: Develop a Shared Compliance Strategy

Good leadership requires you to surround yourself with people of diverse perspectives who can disagree with you without fear of retaliation.

—DORIS KEARNS GOODWIN

If you think of your company as a team of leaders with a hierarchy of board of directors, who are often investors, shareholders, and private equity venture capitalists, etc., all have literally a lot on the line, financially, regarding the success or failure of the company. In addition, you have your executive management team that leads core key functions, such as commercial operations, research and development, finance, marketing, and, of course, we can't leave out the legal aspects and compliance. You have middle management and employees who, at each level, understand and buy into the business strategy, business purpose, and your compliance strategy. With every consensus-building project, effective communication and leadership are imperative.

As mentioned before, the tone at the top is key, and this voice can't be "one and done." You can't do something once, check it off the list, and forget about it. Remember our decision flowchart—choose, monitor, and modify. It is a living, breathing approach. You must continually reinforce compliance regulations through the power of the leader or CEO of the company. Pres. Harry Truman said, "The buck stops here." But it also starts here.

The buck has to start with the CEO, but keep in mind that starting is one thing, but sharing it and developing consensus is another. This is where a CEO likely will need help because the devil is in the details. A seasoned compliance professional can help articulate and present a comprehensive, sensible compliance strategy that is tailored to the culture and operations of your company in a very efficient and timely manner. Of course, while timing is everything and speed is always of the essence, there are times—and this is one of them—where patience is also important. Investing a little bit of time in being thoughtful can yield big dividends and save time down the road.

Many leaders are prone to thinking, "We don't need to spend time doing a risk assessment and reviews because we are starting from scratch. So let's just do it." On the one hand, certainly, that is understandable from a go-getter type of leader—and I consider myself to be one. However, not doing a risk assessment would be a huge mistake because you don't know what you don't know when it comes to compliance. In other words you must know where the weak links are.

A good analogy is if you are boating through a passage to get out to the main lake, you must know where the rocks or any other obstacles are located and be cautious maneuvering through the waterways. Similarly, if you are a skier and like virgin powder snow, if you don't do your homework before you head out, it could be the last run of your life. Smart boaters and skiers look for and know where the crevices and risks are and how to navigate around them to get the most of their experience. The same is true when conducting a compliance risk assessment.

The DOJ has recognized that conducting a compliance risk assessment is perhaps the most important first step for evaluating a compliance program.[31] As we referenced earlier—but it bears repeating to reinforce their importance—for an effective compliance program, the DOJ outlines three fundamental questions:[32]

- Is the compliance program well designed?

- Is the program being applied earnestly or in good faith to function effectively?

- Does the compliance program work in practice?

When you are designing a compliance program, you need to understand the current state of the business and its unique key risks, then create a blueprint. For the life sciences industry, this usually means commercial risk. Why? As we saw earlier, the largest settlements involving billions of dollars have revolved around inappropriate sales and marketing practices. To thwart this risk, interview a cross section of key functional executives and ask them to score key commercial risks that your company may likely face. At TRESTLE Compliance, we have pioneered this risk-scoring process and created proprietary software that generates a heat map juxtaposing vulnerability versus impact when it comes to compliance risk. I will explain its power as a tool here.

VULNERABILITY VERSUS IMPACT

All too often, particularly with start-up life science companies preparing to launch their first product, there is a lack of understanding of key risks. By utilizing such a heat map, you will be able to show a perception gap as we define the x-axis and y-axis. One of them is vulnerability versus impact. Vulnerability measures what you have in place with a compliance risk program that includes the following:

---

31   US Department of Justice Criminal Division, "Evaluation of Corporate Compliance Programs," updated March 2023, 1-2.

32   Ibid.

COMPLIANCE VULNERABILITY
SCORE METHODOLOGY:

0.0–1.0 = Current processes and procedures exist and are included in training and are being followed.

1.1–2.0 = Current processes and procedures exist and are included in training but may or may not be followed.

2.1–3.0 = Processes and procedures exist, there is no training, and may or may not be followed.

3.1–4.0 = No policies and procedures exist for this activity.

Impact refers to the historic impact of the US federal enforcement on a particular risk—the lower the score, the lower the impact, and vice versa. A score of 1.0 means there is no real history of enforcement in this area. A 2.0 means there is relatively minor focus and may trigger an FDA warning letter. A 3.0 is more serious and publicly announces targeted areas of enforcement that have not led to any specific settlements or actions yet.

COMPLIANCE IMPACT SCORE METHODOLOGY:

0.0–1.0 = Activity does not contain historical enforcement risk.

1.1–2.0 = Activity could contain minimal enforcement risk (e.g., FDA letters).

2.1–3.0 = Known/potential targeted enforcement area.

3.1–4.0 = Known/potential targeted enforcement area with history of CIAs, sanctions, and fines.

Here is a sample heat map using this methodology:

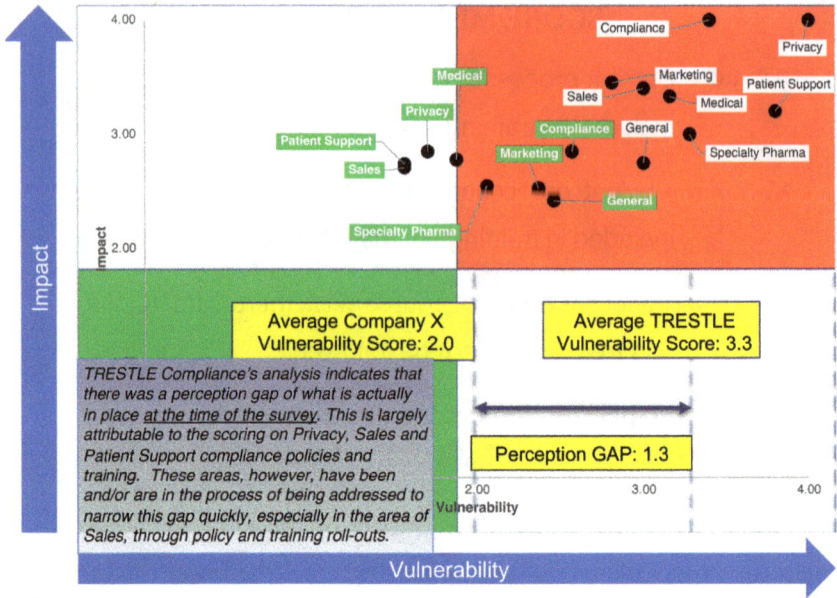

TRESTLE

As mentioned the DOJ has placed significant importance on conducting a risk assessment, stating, "The starting point for a prosecutor's evaluation of whether a company has a well-designed compliance program is to understand the company's business from a commercial perspective, how the company has identified, assessed, and defined its risk profile, and the degree to which the program devotes appropriate scrutiny and resources to the spectrum of risks. In short, prosecutors should endeavor to understand why the company has chosen to set up the compliance program the way that it has, and why and how the company's compliance program has evolved over time."[33]

Bottom line: You need to do a risk assessment, a disciplined process that allows you to identify the risks and gaps so you can fully understand them. Then work to fill in those gaps to create a

---

33   US Department of Justice Criminal Division, "Evaluation of Corporate Compliance Programs," updated March 2023, 2.

comprehensive compliance structure that is risk based and scaled to the size of the company. This saves both time and money, something very important, as the biggest fear that most investors and board members have around compliance is that the program is going to cost a bundle, and therefore, they often put it off or put it on the back burner. This is a big mistake. By not addressing these risks, the risks can grow and eventually cause more damage, especially if something goes wrong. Once you understand your risks with some precision, you can build consensus, support, and understanding about how best to address those risks (read "fund" and "resource") appropriately and the timing to do so (i.e., how to scale up the compliance program with the business in a sensible, cost-effective way and build out your house of compliance). By calibrating and scaling it to your risks, you will save the company time, effort, and costs while making the program more effective both in practice and to outsiders, such as the DOJ and OIG.

Bottom line: An effective compliance program doesn't have to be a big, expensive program; the sooner you get started, the sooner you will identify the risks that will enable you to tailor the program to meet the specific needs of your company.

NEXT STEPS

When you have done your risk assessment and have the results showing that some functions may be in place while others believe less is in place from a compliance perspective, then you know what areas to tackle first. The key is to get a uniform understanding of exactly what is in place and what specific risks may need more attention.

For example, you may need to draft your code of conduct after doing a risk assessment because it might be less or more of what you need to do when it comes to compliance. A risk assessment might show that you have communications and training problems to address. The goal should be to create a baseline of understanding against which you can measure and show progress. Build out your house of compliance and implementation plan so it is specifically tailored to your unique mix of risks and understanding of these risks for your specific business circumstances.

Here are examples of an implementation plan and the "house of compliance" based on Seven Elements:

U.S. Compliance Program Implementation Strategy

We recommend the continuation of the following three-step strategic U.S. Compliance Program Implementation Strategy:

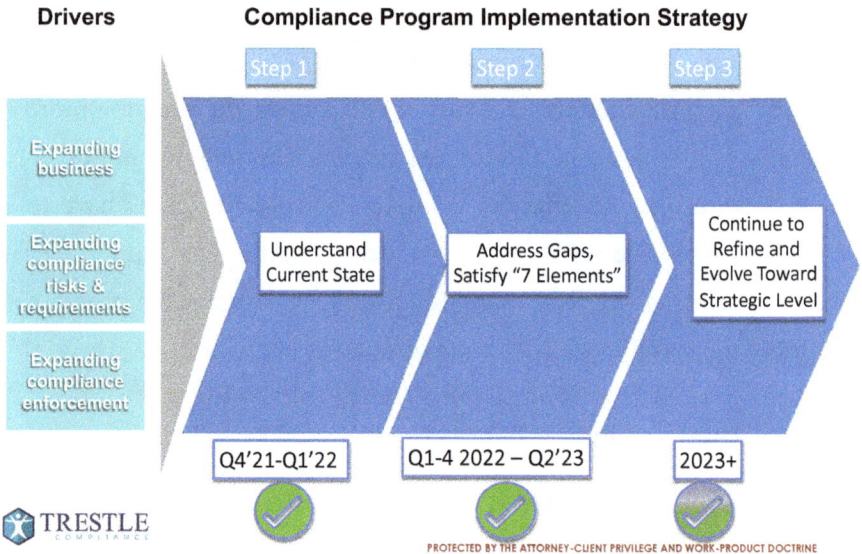

Drivers   **Compliance Program Implementation Strategy**

Step 1 — Understand Current State — Q4'21–Q1'22

Step 2 — Address Gaps, Satisfy "7 Elements" — Q1-4 2022 – Q2'23

Step 3 — Continue to Refine and Evolve Toward Strategic Level — 2023+

Drivers: Expanding business; Expanding compliance risks & requirements; Expanding compliance enforcement

TRESTLE COMPLIANCE

PROTECTED BY THE ATTORNEY-CLIENT PRIVILEGE AND WORK-PRODUCT DOCTRINE

7 Elements of an Effective Compliance Program

Phased Approach with Risk-Prioritized Implementation (Priorities A-D)

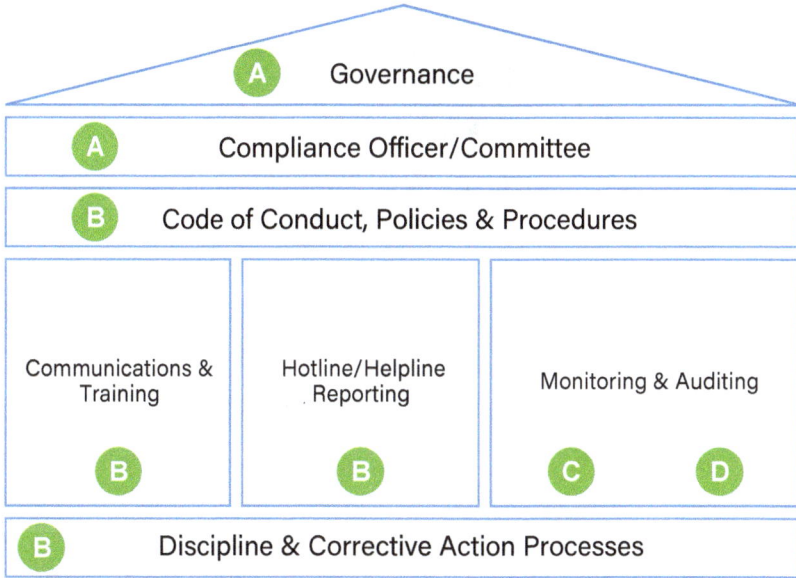

A	Governance
A	Compliance Officer/Committee
B	Code of Conduct, Policies & Procedures
Communications & Training **B**	Hotline/Helpline Reporting **B**	Monitoring & Auditing **C** **D**
B	Discipline & Corrective Action Processes

PRIMA FACIE

Twenty-five years ago, at a conference in Washington, DC, a Department of Treasury attorney suggested that any incidents of noncompliance are prima facie, or "on its face," meaning evidence that the compliance program is not working. This, of course, suggests that the standard of excellence is perfection. Thank goodness this attitude has changed. Now it is all about preventing, detecting, and correcting incidents of misconduct based on your risk, and that is why in 2019 to 2020, the DOJ issued this guidance for prosecutors in evaluating the compliance program when they are considering charging a company with criminal misconduct. The stakes are very high and even more reason to borrow from the old EF Hutton commercial: "When the Department of Justice speaks, people should listen."

Step 3: Map Out a Detailed Shared Execution Plan

It takes less time to do a thing right than to explain why you did it wrong.

—HENRY WADSWORTH
LONGFELLOW

When it comes to executing your compliance program, you must define who does what. Who are the key stakeholders that will determine success or failure? Larry Bossidy, who wrote the book *Execution*, points out that you can strategize and plan, plan, and plan, but at the end of the day, it is the action that matters. Doing so means executing against the plan, though it is not perfect, but you have a mindset of time is pressure. The longer you do not have a compliance program in place, the greater risk you have that something can go wrong. It is important to get the show on the road and be willing to accept that being at 80 percent in terms of policies, procedures, development, and consensus with the team is where you want to be.

Time is a critical factor that can affect your success, so you want to have a mindset of execution, moving forward, and getting the Seven Elements in place. It is like building a house and putting the roof on so you can get out of the rain. Once that has taken place, you can continue to improve it and make it better, as opposed to making it perfect before you move in. Basically, there is no other alternative; you are either outside in the cold and elements or inside feeling safe and secure to reduce your risks.

Another best-selling book on this is *Thinking, Fast and Slow* by the late Daniel Kahneman, PhD, a professor of psychology at Princeton University who was awarded the Nobel Memorial Prize in Economic

Sciences and was the 2012 winner of the National Academies Communication award for best creative work that helps people understand behavioral science, engineering, and medicine. In his pioneering work of decision-making, he points out that people are prone to biases, preferences, and preconceptions.

When it comes to risk, depending on their personality and makeup, people often overestimate risk and are overconfident, or they underestimate risk and expose themselves to unnecessary danger. We need to account for this and factor it in when it comes to compliance. You can be too conservative on the one hand and unrealistic on the other hand and, in the process, create unnecessary risk. Providing the business with a risk-based analysis, where as a compliance officer, you share with them a continuum of risk from low to medium to high, and depending on where they are on that spectrum, their actions will follow.

As we mentioned, often, there is no black and white, right or wrong, when it comes to things that have never been tried before. Ultimately, a compliance program should be able to answer a question that has never been asked before. In other words you must always be looking ahead and be proactive in providing compliance guidance. That is where a keen, sharp, and thorough understanding of regulations and enforcement is critical to provide the capability of accurately assessing any current set of circumstances and project into the future as to how acceptable or unacceptable proposed actions may be from a compliance perspective. This is where a risk analysis is critically important.

For example, currently in the life sciences industry, many companies are pursuing therapies in the rare disease market. These therapies are high cost, require a lot of patient education and support, and trigger potential new antikickback scenarios that may not have occurred in the past. There is an inherent tension in providing appropriate patient support that has value while, on the other hand, may appear to be an inducement to use the product to skeptical outsiders.

This is where an overconservative approach, in my opinion, would be to simply say "No, you can't do that." Such an answer will likely create a grudging backlash against compliance, a future pattern of avoiding the tough questions from compliance, and perhaps even a secretive work-around against the compliance recommendation. The alternative and recommended approach is to do the intellectually challenging and difficult heavy lifting of teasing out the critical factors that can tip the balance from compliant to noncompliant behavior and lay that out from a risk perspective for the business and give them options based on that risk analysis. This should provide the appropriate information that demonstrates due diligence from a compliance perspective while at the same time empowering business leaders to make well-informed risk-based decisions.

As a compliance officer, you may be posed with requests from the commercial team in ethically gray areas. *How does that come into play?*

An effective compliance program comes down to good judgment, effective decision-making, and putting in checks and balances to correct any kind of illegal or inappropriate actions by employees of the company. It all starts with the executive team and CEO's good judgment, engaging the board, sharing case studies that not only challenge them but also guard against any over- or underestimation when it comes to risk.

Take for example Abraham Lincoln, who had to deal with his Civil War cabinet members, a disparate group of competitors that he purposefully brought together for differing points of view and perspectives that guarded against his own potential biases. Known to be a decisive leader, he did not rely on information that was twice removed and made a point of speaking to as many people as possible. He was also known for his integrity and willingness to do the right thing even if it was unpopular or difficult. In his decision-making process, he used checks and balances with information to make the best possible judgment at any given moment.

When it comes to execution with compliance and appropriate decision-making from a company-wide perception, you must create a mindset that starts with the top leader. Know that you are not going to be paralyzed in the pursuit of perfection but driven by excellence. Stay grounded to take action in a timely fashion in the imperfect world we live in because we can't wait for perfection. Compliance is not about perfection (which would be impossible); it is about putting in place the proper controls, mindset, and *inspiration* to align a group of people to act within certain boundaries to reach certain goals in an ethical manner, especially in the life sciences arena, where people's lives are at stake. Principal-based leadership is driven by values that are reinforced with the following:

- Communication

- Documentation

- Training

- Leadership by example

With any team, whether it is a corporation, sports team, or military team, success requires a clear understanding of what needs to be done, who does what, and what their role is. And just as specifically what—or how—does their role contribute to achieving the goals of the team? That's achieved by showing respect for each individual role and explaining the why behind the what. As a result you get buy-in and motivate everyone to perform their role to their very best, in fact, beyond their best. This is what great coaches, leaders, and parents do:

they get people to perform beyond their own expectations. That is how you win with compliance and propel performance.

SPECIFIC TECHNIQUES FOR COMPLIANCE OFFICERS

➜ *Develop Your Compliance Brand*

Compliance is a service that should add value. Each organization is unique, and the compliance service it requires should reflect a unique value proposition. The word "compliance" alone, as we have shared earlier, triggers negative reactions in the hearts and minds of most people. To counterbalance that, creating a positive compliance brand is essential. Some compliance branding examples I have used and created over the years include the following:

- "Acting on Our Values" for TAP Pharmaceuticals

- "Winning with Compliance" for Warner Chilcott

- "Succeeding with Compliance" for Cycle Pharmaceuticals

- "Innovation Through Integrity" for Theratechnologies

Branding your compliance program is important for the same reason branding any product or service; it creates a way to trigger a unique recognition of what you want compliance to represent in the minds of your target audience. As with any brand, you need to pull it through in different ways, whether that be a booth with the brand and logo at a national sales meeting, a logo that is at the footer of every email, a logo on PowerPoint slides and presentations. You get the idea. You want to reinforce the brand with every possible interaction with your target audience.

➜ *Provide Specific Solutions to Specific Problems and Questions*

Perhaps the number one source of frustration for consumers of legal and compliance services is that answers to concerns or questions are too vague. For example, salespeople in particular really like things to be black and white, and while that isn't always possible, to the degree that you can provide clear guidance, do so. Clarity, when possible, will be greatly appreciated, and you will win credibility by giving real answers to real questions. A solid compliance program will also build your reputational capital when gray areas or questions arise. People will be more willing to listen to you and work with you in the "gray zone" if you can provide the black-and-white answers when possible.

Again, it is about building trust over the long run.

➜ *Be Responsive*

Perhaps this should be number two—or tied for number one and equally a source of frustration: lawyers and compliance professionals take forever to provide an answer. While no one suggests that you should rush in answering a difficult compliance question, even a simple acknowledgment such as "Yes, I received your question. Let me get back to you by tomorrow or next week," or whatever is appropriate. A quick note goes a long way in keeping your credibility intact and your customers happy. Here again, following the golden rule is truly the guide. If you like it when people get back to you quickly, then certainly, you should try to do the same for others.

A key to responsiveness is managing your client's or audience's expectations. Be conservative when making timing estimates so that you can overdeliver consistently. Of course, things happen, and when they do, people will be much more understanding when being late is the exception and not the rule. Deliver results consistently on time.

Another key to responsiveness is putting in metrics and applying operational management techniques for compliance-related operations (e.g., for measuring turnaround time and staying within certain time frames for answering questions). In other words help establish compliance as a well-managed professional function.

➔ *Always Be Respectful and Courteous*

Certainly, there may be times when the frustrations of any given day may get the best of you. Compliance is a tough job, and sometimes, it is wiser to take a deep breath, count to ten, or even sleep on an issue before giving a complete answer. You cannot allow your emotions to dictate your response or affect your decision-making. The damage you will do to your credibility in perhaps one email or one rude comment will take you weeks, if not months, to recover. A word to the wise: know yourself when you are tired and fatigued or when you are under stress because that is when you are most prone to making a mistake. Don't kid yourself, compliance is an extremely high-stress job, and you will be in that situation often.

➔ *Have a Sense of Humor*

Compliance is serious enough day-to-day, and as I have shared, most people understandably tend to dread the topic. Find ways that are appropriate to lighten it up a bit. Usually, self-deprecating humor can work in your favor, but a word of caution about humor and compliance: don't overdo it. Compliance is a serious topic for good reason, and you shouldn't try to negate that. I have seen people overdo it and lose credibility. I have also seen well-intended humor fall flat because it was with the wrong audience at the wrong time. Know your audience and the situation and use humor where appropriate and sparingly, but use it to your advantage to connect with your audience.

➜ *Stay Curious and Practice "Intellectual Arbitrage"*

Regardless of what industry you are in, you can always learn from other industries. That certainly applies to compliance as well. The principles and core practices of effective compliance are the same across industries. The specific challenges, practical experiences, and lessons learned, however, may vary. Attend cross-industry compliance conferences and learn how other industries have tackled certain issues that perhaps your industry has not. I did this myself and learned how the defense and financial services industry struggled earlier with a very legalistic approach to compliance codes of conduct, policies, and training.

Step 4: Execute Your Plan Collaboratively

Unity is strength ... when there is teamwork and collaboration, wonderful things can be achieved.

—MATTIE STEPANEK

Most modern companies and teams are built on the concept of collaboration. Gone are the days of strict hierarchical authoritarian corporate environments. While some may still remain, my guess is that they will not be around for long. With the emphasis on imagination, diversity, inclusion, ideas, and of course, execution, it takes a real team to put it all together. Compliance should reflect these same values and work collaboratively with all other team members. By doing so, you will generate trust and respect as someone who truly is looking out for what is best for the team.

It is critically important to signal that compliance is not locked into preconceived answers and solutions. Rather, compliance reflects an open and nimble mind, receptive to change that makes sense and that can be defended. This is where value-driven leadership makes all the difference because, ultimately, values should always drive the underlying mission. In the life sciences context, putting the health and safety of patients first and foremost is the right thing to do both morally, ethically, and professionally. And when we do so, the legal compliance piece naturally falls into place.

By contrast, if you lead with a heavy hand and a "do it or else" threat because specific policies and procedures are what is required by the law, people will resist and fight you on it. It really is quite simple; collaboration is a key to success and winning with compliance. Creating a product or service in the life sciences industry requires combing a sequence of tasks and smart decisions to ensure that a product or service is of the highest quality, is safe for the patient, and meets compliance standards.

In most cases the strongest business processes are those that take advantage of combining compliance with collaboration. Consistency and improved efficiency are the result of combining good business decisions with teamwork and transparency. When you combine compliance rules and processes into a single source of truth, you create a business model that operates with specific compliance responsibilities that do the following:

- Allow for better control

- Offer efficient response to any changes

- Help identify future opportunities

In essence, all things work better together.

THE BENEFITS OF COLLABORATION

Approaching compliance requirements, rules, and regulations in a collaborative way helps integrate compliance into the corporate DNA and the culture of the company. By integrating compliance in this way, it allows for more effective and less disruptive change management when needed and a natural reemphasis on quality management. Compliance is quality, and quality is compliance.

Creating this nexus generates the pride and confidence in business owners, stakeholders, and board members to credibly reassure patients and customers that the work, product, or service is completed correctly the first time every time. From an employee's perspective, integrating a compliance program directly into your business model creates a single source of truth, honesty, and transparency for people to work better, faster, and with confidence that they are meeting the requirements of the business in a compliance manner. Compliance should be a desired by-product of good business processes, not necessarily the reason or focus of the process. Effective compliance programs align and integrate compliance into the business to support the business, not the other way around.

Collaboration is key. It is how everyone helps each other to make the whole greater than the sum of its parts. Whether rowing on a crew team as I did or working at a biotech company to bring a new therapy to market to help patients with a rare disease, working together as a well-oiled machine is what delivers success and propels performance.

Step 5: Measure and Report Your Results

Records management is knowing what you have, where
you have it, and how long you have to keep it.

—ANONYMOUS

Any well-run organization knows that it is critically important to measure and report results. The compliance function should be no different. Establishing key performance indicators by developing a clear board of directors and executive-level dashboard means establishing defined work plans with time frames, deadlines, and roles and responsibilities. Of course, managing a budget and reporting results are essential for business credibility. An effective compliance program should be managed as a business process. Simply developing and executing a strategy is not enough.

A critical and necessary component of a successful compliance program is *measuring and reporting results*. Capturing feedback from your customers through surveys, interviews, and focus groups is highly recommended for both the front-end development stage and the back-end feedback stage.

For example, multidimensional metrics can enable a company or organization to better understand the root causes of issues related to retention, engagement, and attitude. Measuring results can also look at the time needed to close audit issues and the number of repeat audit issues, client or customer satisfaction, or complaints at the business level. These metrics also provide insights into compliance effectiveness.

Closing the loop in this manner ensures continued connectivity and relevance to the audience you intend to serve. It allows you to quantify and measure results and to demonstrate measurable improvement and progress over time. Depicting these results graphically and reporting them to the company's executive team and board again reinforces the notion that the compliance program is indeed a well-managed business process and partner that is adding tangible value to the business.

At the end of the day, however, as with any successful business or venture, the success of a compliance program hinges on the performance of the people who are, indeed, the compliance department. Starting at the top of the department with the chief compliance officer down through the ranks, consistent, quality interactions over time that keep promises made and deliver results—these are the building blocks of trust upon which the reputation of the program stands.

ACCURATE COMPLIANCE RECORDS

A good compliance program ensures that the records management policies and procedures are followed and that you are in line with any retention schedules required by law. When a company or organization is audited by a government entity, compliance with the applicable laws is one of the items that need to be verified and confirmed. It is critical to have accurate and complete compliance records that support all documentation for payments and transactions, charges, and all costs that include the following:

- Receipts

- Reports

- Analyses

- Filings

- Data including emails and electronic data

- All information created, collected, processed, and stored

This is the case where the devil is in the details, and you cannot afford to let any of these details slip.

EFFECTIVE RECORDS MANAGEMENT SYSTEM

All the items listed previously, plus policies, procedures, and activities within an organization or business, are required to implement an effective and efficient records management system. There are six foundational elements to include:

- Records Inventory and Classification

- Retention Scheduling

- Records Storage and Conversion
- Vital Records Program
- Disaster Prevention and Recovery Planning
- Disposition

Having a complete records management system in place can reduce operating costs, save money, and improve the efficiency of all employees and staff with access to information they need to work efficiently and be productive. It also allows easy access to pertinent information that facilitates making informed decisions when needed.

FOUR STEPS TO CREATE AN EFFECTIVE RECORDS MANAGEMENT PROGRAM

An effective policies and procedures system sets the standard for an effective compliant records management system. It should contain the management of all records, including paper, email, and texts. Your business should have separate policies for active and unused files, retaining all records, including emails, and have a system in place for managing information.

An effective program will include the following steps:

- Complete an inventory of all your records.

- Determine the person who is going to manage the process and records.
- Develop a records retention and destruction schedule.
- Determine the best way to store and manage all records.

By taking your records management program seriously, it will allow a more effective means of managing your current records (both electronic and paper), reduce or eliminate redundant recordkeeping, reduce costs of storage equipment and supplies, and eliminate unnecessary files.

An effective records management system ensures that your business can gain access to reliable evidence if required by law to justify your actions or defend your position. Therefore, it is essential that a sound, cost-effective business case can be formulated to support the investment required to maintain an efficient records management program.

Now, as we near the end of the book, let's take a look toward the future. Artificial intelligence, block chain technology, and a future heavy with data, tech, and innovations we cannot yet fully imagine are upon us. Those of us concerned with compliance will have to continue to evolve and adapt and address these changes, some of which will cause seismic shifts in how we do things. However, as I have emphasized again and again, we must never forget the core principles of effective leadership.

CHAPTER 8:

WHAT'S NEXT?—FUTURE COMPLIANCE RISKS OF LIFE SCIENCES

*Even the most rational approach to ethics is defenseless
if there isn't the will to do what is right.*

—ALBERT SOLZHENITSYN

n the above quote, one might even argue that, in this case, the rational approach risks becoming the unethical one. Since the 1970s and Watergate, the adage, "Follow the money!" has summed up what government investigators do to crack a case. For example, in 1992, the Clinton administration declared war on healthcare fraud, as discussed earlier. For over three decades, this "endless war" has continued regardless of administration.

Why? Because there is more money than ever in the system, and this war spilled into the pharmaceutical and life sciences sector. While the COVID-19 pandemic put a slight pause on enforcement activity, a Special Fraud Alert for Speaker Programs from the OIG in

2020 signaled an unprecedented warning that stricter oversight and enforcement are here for the foreseeable future.

Generally, like much of government and politics, the approach toward compliance is cyclical. Under Republican administrations, there is usually less regulation and less pursuit in that area. Under Democratic administrations, the opposite is often true. Regardless of who sits in the Oval Office, from a government perspective, the war on healthcare fraud is both good politics and good economics. It demonstrates concerted government action to safeguard federal taxpayer dollars and concern for the most vulnerable in our society, including those who are sick, the elderly, and children. Plus, it also holds crooks accountable while recovering billions of dollars in settlements for the federal treasury. This is not a bad business model if you are the government. Big settlements make big news—the optics can be very good for the government when they go after large-scale fraud. Go big or go home applies here too!

The multiplier effects of the pandemic, combined with healthcare initiatives implemented by the Biden–Harris administration, guaranteed a commensurate launch of a new era of healthcare fraud enforcement. In fiscal year 2023, the DOJ continued building its track record of record enforcement activity, with False Claims Act settlements and judgments exceeding $2.68 billion from a record 543 settlements and judgments, the highest number of settlements and judgments in a single year in history.[34] Regardless of which party wins the next election, or the one after that, the government will continue to "follow the money," which will continue to lead them straight to healthcare and the life sciences industry.

Quite simply, unprecedented times of innovation, leaps in AI, big data, research, and technology create unprecedented risks for

---

34   US Department of Justice, Office of Public Affairs Press Release, February 22, 2024.

fraud and abuse and an associated need for accountability, oversight, and enforcement. As I earlier quoted former attorney general Dick Thornburgh, when the DOJ makes any issue a priority, two things are guaranteed to happen: more prosecutions and more convictions.

As the national priority shifted to guiding a COVID-19 recovery, both medically and economically, the life sciences industry remained in laser focus both nationally and globally. The takeaway: a lot of money is on the line, and life sciences companies need to take compliance very seriously if they want to stay ahead of the game in this fast-changing, high-risk environment. Though the COVID-19 pandemic is over, this will surely not be our only global health crisis. Those in life sciences need to be ready.

Knowing this makes updating the risk profile of your ethics and compliance program more important than ever. If your organization doesn't have a plan to stay ahead of these developments, the time is now to develop one immediately. If you do have one in place, be sure to follow through with implementation. Additionally, it's paramount to stay vigilant and on top of new legislative, regulatory, and enforcement developments coming from the federal government; these are likely to change rapidly as new officials take their posts and start implementing new priorities to make their mark—whether the administration at the time of this writing or the next one.

Staying fresh on current DOJ, OIG, and FDA guidelines and staying on top of newly or recently issued ones, such as the OIG "General Compliance Program Guidance" (CPG) and the planned release of improved and updated industry-specific CPGs, or the FDA's draft guidance issued in October 2023 titled "Communications from Firms to Health Care Providers Regarding Scientific Information on Unapproved Uses of Approved/Cleared Medical Products Questions and Answers," are all critically important to understand and incorporate into any compliance program.

Getting compliance right is critical as risks are changing and growing. As businesses have opened back up post-COVID-19, there remains an added premium on communication, collaboration, and coordination among executives, compliance/privacy officers, and sales teams.

By following this advice, smart companies will successfully see over the horizon and avoid being caught in the crosshairs of a new batch of federal investigators under a new or continuing administration looking to make names for themselves by identifying viable targets of enforcement opportunity.

In short, the life sciences industry is booming, with billions of dollars flowing in, giving rise to added compliance risks and enforcement. A thoughtful compliance strategy will anticipate the added risks of increased focus on compliance, depending on the focus of whatever administration is leading the country, and position your company to continue to compete and win aggressively in the marketplace. Your continued credible investment in integrity and the mission of your company will continue to inspire the integrity of your employees to want to comply. Again, that is how you will *win with compliance and propel performance.*

With every new administration, we look for important priorities in the drivers for compliance. For example, drug pricing has been one of the hottest issues relating to the pharmaceutical industry; it is an issue that has been discussed by Congress since 1986. However, nothing much has really happened. The Trump administration made some bold attempts to address drug pricing, and the Biden administration raised it as an important issue as well. Clearly, drug pricing cuts across all demographics and partisan lines, yet not much has happened. Why? The answer is that the drug industry lobby has always been powerful and now, post-COVID-19 pandemic, it is more powerful than ever.

On the one hand, the drug industry has really stepped up in a big way by creating remarkably effective vaccines in record time to help the world get back to a new normal.

As I previously mentioned, in 2020 the OIG issued a Special Fraud Alert on speaker programs using unprecedented sharp and clear language. The OIG warned the life sciences industry of its great skepticism regarding speaker programs and put the industry on clear notice that using speaker programs meant engaging in high-risk behavior.

The second area affected is the contract sales forces, who will come under greater scrutiny. Smaller companies continue to outsource their entire sales forces with checks and balances to compliant behavior, but they may become subject to questionable activity. This is reflected in a DOJ memorandum that identifies a concern with contract sales forces regarding pushing their products into the market, commissions based on percentage of sales, and direct contact between the sales agent and the physicians in a position to order items or services that are then paid for by a federal healthcare program.

For example, the United States Fourth Circuit Court of Appeals affirmed a $114 million judgment against three defendants found liable for defrauding Medicare and TRICARE. At trial, the United States contended that when specialty labs Health Diagnostics Laboratory, Inc. and Singulex Inc. paid commissions to their marketing firm, Bluewave, based on the number of blood tests sold, the parties violated the Anti-Kickback Statute. The United States argued these volume-based commissions constituted "remuneration" intended to induce Bluewave's sales representatives to sell as many blood tests as possible.

The United States also contended the Anti-Kickback Statute prohibited Bluewave from paying its salespeople for recommending the tests. By paying these kickbacks, the defendants caused false claims to be submitted to federal healthcare programs for millions of dollars in unnecessary blood tests. The jury agreed, and the Fourth Circuit affirmed the jury's verdict in a published opinion.

This is an important victory for American taxpayers, patients, and the Medicare program showing that anyone who schemes to defraud our federal healthcare system will be held accountable for their actions. Though the defendants were warned by outside lawyers about the illegality of the commissions, the ruling sends a strong message as a deterrent that this sort of conduct will not be tolerated. Kickbacks undermine the public's trust in the healthcare system and the integrity of federal healthcare programs.[35]

CORRUPTION

Putting specific laws and statutes to the side for now, a core global concern that has been growing over the past several decades is corruption. Governmental, political, global, and financial corruption play an overall distorting and tainting influence of money on society. When it comes to compliance, one must face corruption head-on in the life sciences industry, which is at the very core of government enforcement and regulation.

Unlike other countries such as the United Kingdom, in the United States, we have different laws to address this one area of corruption. Specifically, on the domestic front, the federal Anti-Kickback Act is, in essence, our domestic anticorruption law. At its heart, it is an anticorruption statute designed to protect federal healthcare program

---

35   The published opinion *U.S. v. LaTonya Mallory et al., No. 18-1811*, filed February 22, 2021. Here is the link to the March DOJ press release: https://www.justice.gov/usao-sc/pr/fourth-circuit-court-appeals-affirms-114-million-judgment-against-3-defendants-found.

beneficiaries from the influence of money on referral decisions and therefore is intended to guard against increased costs, overutilization, and poor-quality services. For life sciences companies in particular, numerous touchpoints with government or employees have increased government scrutiny and allegations that companies have engaged in pay-to-prescribe and pay-to-play schemes. The COVID-19 pandemic increased pressure on the life sciences industry to address new challenges and has ultimately introduced new risks around bribery and corruption activity.

Internationally, the US law is the Foreign Corrupt Practices Act (FCPA), which addresses the corruption of foreign government officials. The FCPA was enacted for the purpose of making it unlawful for certain classes of persons and entities to make payments to foreign government officials to assist in obtaining or retaining business. In healthcare this becomes relevant because most HCPs, such as physicians, are employees of government-run health systems, qualifying them as "foreign government officials" under the FCPA.

In the United Kingdom, there is one law to address both domestic and foreign corruption, the UK antibribery/anticorruption law (the Bribery Act of 2010). As an executive and investor of a life sciences company, or any company for that matter, it is important to appreciate that any transfer of value has the potential, in fact or appearance, to be a bribe. You need to know how to distinguish between a valid transaction and an illegal one. This is where a compliance program needs to explain the why behind the what. Understanding this core concept that government follows the money because whether in this country or other countries, there is a long history of bribes and corruption to gain influence and to profit.

To distill it down to a simple test whenever you are paying anyone for anything, please ask yourself, "Why are we doing this?" You need to readily look yourself in the mirror and say, "The reason is credible, legitimate, and appropriate."

All too often, executives and companies have gotten into trouble by rationalizing payments, benefits, or giveaways, all in the name of patient care and service. The reality, unfortunately in some past cases, was these transfers of value were simply to induce more prescriptions for more profit.

Also, beware of "incrementalism." It is too easy to go down a slippery slope of allowing small transgressions that then snowball into larger ones. I have heard more than once, for example, that embezzlers often start out small, thinking they will repay whatever it is they "borrowed." As time goes on and they are unable to pay increasing amounts back, the embezzlement evolves. In the compliance world, it can be much the same. You, as a compliance officer, must not tolerate incrementalism and must know where the bright line is—the Rubicon that cannot be crossed.

That said, there are notable and legitimate reasons to consider new options to enhance patient support and care, especially in the rare disease market, but this is not always black and white. That said, don't discourage executives and investors to stop thinking outside the box or about how they can further enhance patient care through appropriate services together with pharmaceutical products.

It is important to appreciate the level of scrutiny and enforcement that the United States has taken relative to foreign corruption and enforcement of the FCPA over the past ten to fifteen years. You will see in the table below the series of settlements and enforcement actions that have been taken by the DOJ in this area from 1978 through 2023. You see that really until 2008, very little, if any, enforcement action occurred. But a veritable explosion of enforcement ensued from 2008 with a peak hit in 2020.

TOTAL SETTLEMENTS BY YEAR

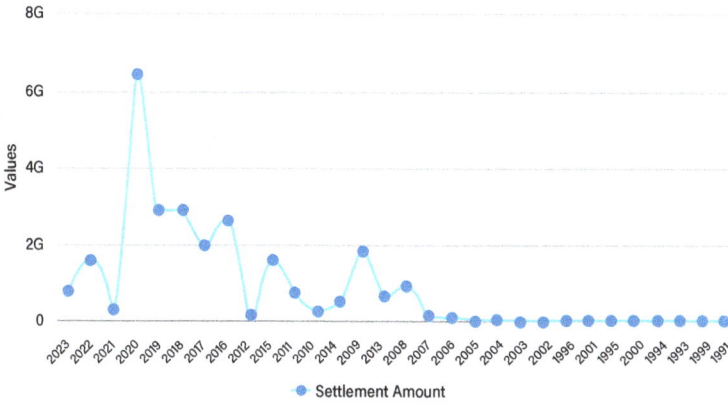

BREAKDOWN BY TOTAL SETTLEMENTS PAID

Public vs. Private

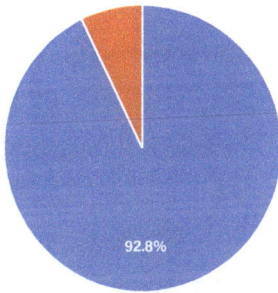

Public
Private

HQ Country

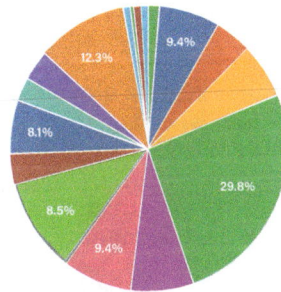

Sweden · Brazil
Russia · France
United Kingdom · Japan
United States · Switzerland
Germany · Israel
South Korea · Singapore

Table courtesy of the FCPA Blog (see https://fcpablog.com)

The government and public are as skeptical as ever of the intentions of companies and individuals when it comes to corruption and bribery. Unfortunately, these settlements depict a world where that skepticism is well founded and documented. Accordingly, even though your company may have the highest standards of integrity, it is important to demonstrate and articulate that to your employees and customers clearly, credibly, and consistently. If you do so, you will succeed in setting yourself apart in a way that will be both personally and financially rewarding. Employees are proud to be part of a company that opposes corruption. This will reduce your risks, inspire integrity, and allow you to win with compliance and propel performance.

ARTIFICIAL INTELLIGENCE AND BLOCKCHAIN TECHNOLOGY

The twenty-first century will be a century of unprecedented technological advancement. Fueling that advancement is artificial intelligence and blockchain technology.

When it comes to compliance and financial transactions, it is likely that AI and blockchain technology will become central components of an effective global compliance program. They will be the specific indication of a broader concept that no compliance program of the future will be effective without a technological component. The requirements and demands for real-time information, credible and consistent checks and balances, and the need to monitor and audit quickly, effectively, and thoroughly are only going to increase.

Accordingly, I have strived to combine "the best thoughtware with the best software" as a compliance consultant for my clients, and I see this combination becoming a requirement in the future. In other words software programs to support and complement your compliance team will not be optional. As discussed earlier, the DOJ and OIG have made their expectations clear as well with regard to compliance data analytic capabilities they expect from organizations in their updated compliance guidances. We must advance with the times.

With regard to AI, the clearest and perhaps most easily foreseeable application, from a compliance perspective, is in monitoring and auditing. Understanding and identifying key factors of risk, when plugged into an AI model, will help identify specific areas of business operations that should be monitored and audited. This will enhance the ability of any compliance program to not only accurately detect noncompliance but also deter noncompliance. Another application of AI also may be in the area of drafting policies, procedures, and training content. Of course, a word of caution here: the key word is "drafting." While AI may be able to produce a credible draft in mere seconds, saving tremendous time, effort, and cost, any AI-generated document, especially in the world of legal compliance, needs to be carefully reviewed, cross-checked, and edited for accuracy by a trained and qualified human professional. You can't just rely on technology; you need both software and thoughtware!

In life sciences as a whole, artificial intelligence will have a seismic impact, just as it will on all aspects of our lives. With respect to the life sciences and pharmaceutical industries, AI is poised to usher in an era of unprecedented advancements in drug discovery, personalized medicine, clinical trials, and patient care. AI's future role in these sectors is set to enhance efficiency, accuracy, and innovation, addressing some of the most significant challenges faced by the industry today.

In terms of drug discovery and development, traditional methods of drug discovery are time consuming and costly, often taking over a decade and billions of dollars to bring a new drug to market. AI can dramatically accelerate this process by analyzing vast datasets to identify potential drug candidates, predict their efficacy, and optimize their chemical structures. Machine learning algorithms can sift through millions of compounds, assessing their potential interactions with biological targets, thus identifying promising candidates much faster than conventional methods.

AI is also set to play a pivotal role in the advancement of personalized medicine, which aims to tailor medical treatment to individual characteristics. By leveraging AI to analyze genetic, environmental, and lifestyle data, healthcare providers can develop personalized treatment plans that are more effective and have fewer side effects. AI-driven platforms can integrate and interpret complex datasets from genomics, proteomics, and metabolomics, providing insights into how different patients will respond to various treatments. This capability is crucial for diseases such as cancer, where AI can help identify the most effective treatment options based on a patient's unique genetic makeup.

The application of AI in clinical trials is another area with transformative potential. Clinical trials are essential for the development of new therapies but are often hampered by high costs, lengthy durations, and recruitment challenges. AI can optimize the design and execution of clinical trials by predicting patient recruitment and retention rates, identifying suitable trial participants through advanced data analysis, and monitoring patient data in real time to ensure safety and efficacy. Additionally, AI can help in adaptive trial designs, which allow for modifications to the trial protocol based on interim results, thereby improving efficiency and success rates. It is already accelerating the clinical trial process.[36]

AI's role extends into patient care and monitoring, where it can enhance the management of chronic diseases, improve diagnostic accuracy, and facilitate remote patient monitoring. AI-powered tools can analyze data from wearable devices and electronic health records

---

36   Matthew Hutson, "How AI Is Being Used to Accelerate Clinical Trials," Nature News, March 13, 2024, https://www.nature.com/articles/d41586-024-00753-x.

to provide continuous monitoring of patients, alerting healthcare providers to potential issues before they become critical. For example, AI algorithms can detect early signs of diseases such as diabetes and cardiovascular conditions, enabling timely intervention and better disease management.

Now comes the caution. As AI becomes more integrated into the life sciences industry, it is crucial to address ethical and regulatory considerations. Ensuring the transparency and explanation of AI algorithms is essential to gain trust from HCPs and patients who may be subject to them. Regulatory frameworks need to evolve to keep pace with technological advancements, providing clear guidelines on the use of AI in drug development and patient care. Additionally, safeguarding patient data privacy and security remains a priority, requiring robust measures to prevent data breaches and misuse.

Looking ahead, the integration of AI with other emerging technologies such as blockchain, the Internet of Things (IoT), and advanced robotics promises to further enhance its impact on life sciences and pharmaceuticals. For example, AI combined with blockchain can ensure the integrity and traceability of pharmaceutical supply chains, while AI-driven IoT devices can enable more sophisticated remote monitoring systems.

BLOCKCHAIN TECHNOLOGY CONTRACTS AND TRANSACTIONS

Similarly, regarding blockchain technology, the clearest and most foreseeable application from a compliance perspective will be in the area of contracts and transactions. Given that contracts with HCPs that transfer value have historically been among the highest risk areas from a commercial compliance perspective, the rigor and certainty that blockchain technology provides in ensuring that contract terms are adhered to by all parties and that contracts and all transactions can be readily audited will provide a new standard of assurance. This will significantly reduce risks and violations moving forward.

Blockchain technologies can improve private regulatory compliance, but blockchain can also help regulators. This is possible because blockchain technology lends itself to the improvement of compliance processes, as it can be used to help compliance officers keep track of the steps required by complex regulations.

Blockchain technology is inherently secure because of a combination of its decentralized architecture, consensus mechanisms, cryptographic techniques, and immutable recordkeeping. The decentralized nature of blockchain means that it operates on a network of nodes, each holding a copy of the entire blockchain. This eliminates a single point of failure and makes it incredibly difficult for attackers to alter the data, as they would need to control a majority of the network simultaneously. Consensus mechanisms such as Proof of Work and Proof of Stake ensure that transactions are validated and recorded only after solving complex mathematical problems or staking significant assets, respectively, making fraudulent activities highly resource-intensive and economically unfeasible. Cryptographic hashing links each block to the previous one, creating a secure chain where altering a single block would require remining all subsequent blocks. This process, combined with digital signatures, ensures data integrity and authenticity. The immutability of the blockchain means that once a transaction is recorded, it cannot be altered without affecting all subsequent blocks, further securing the data. Additionally, the transparency of public blockchains allows continuous auditing by the community, quickly exposing any malicious activity. Redundancy is another security layer, as the distributed nature of blockchain ensures data replication across many nodes, maintaining the network's integrity even if some nodes are compromised. Smart contracts add further security by automating and enforcing agreements without human intervention, reducing the risk of fraud and errors. Finally, the open-source nature of many blockchain projects invites a global community of developers to continuously review and enhance the code, rapidly identifying and fixing vulnerabilities. These combined features create a robust, tamper-proof system, making blockchain technology one of the most secure digital solutions available.

We are going to be hearing more and more about this in the compliance world. In fact, these new changes are all the more reason to be sure you have a compliance sherpa who is keeping on top of these rapid developments.

Why You Should Conduct a Compliance Risk Assessment *Now*

With this new mix of compliance risk upon us, now is the time to reassess how they are affecting your life sciences company.

Without a specialized understanding of the specific risks for your particular company, therapeutic area, and products, chances are high that you're going to miss something. With the convergence of commercial activity and data security/privacy risks means it's time to look in the mirror and be honest: Do you truly understand your mix of vulnerabilities and how to quantify and prioritize them? If the answer is no, conducting a compliance risk assessment is a sensible, powerful solution.

As we have discussed, per the DOJ, administering a compliance risk assessment is the "starting point"—the single most important first step your company can and should take in implementing an effective compliance program.[37] If you've never commissioned one, doing so as soon as possible should be a key part of your commercial compliance strategy. If it's been two or more years since your most recent "risk physical," an update now is imperative. Even if you've conducted one more recently, staying current is critical.

Whenever circumstances change for you or your business, such as you've joined a new company as the new GC, COO, or chief compliance officer; new products are launched; you've made new acquisitions; or gone through a once-in-a-century pandemic (imagine that!), it's time for a "booster shot" to protect yourself against potential risks through a bespoke compliance risk assessment that lays the foundation for future commercial health and success.

The temptation with anything in life, however, is to avoid doing any initial screening because we might learn things we don't like. We are tempted to say, "Let's just get on with it!" Getting a baseline report, whether it's for your physical health or the health of your business, can identify important hazards. Doing so is both wise and prudent. Like getting a CT scan, it is a rational way of identifying, targeting, quantifying, and prioritizing risks *with precision* so you can successfully respond, adapt, and continue to operate effectively. Protecting yourself, whether from the flu or COVID-19 or the new emerging mix of compliance risks, makes *abundant rational sense.*

Compliance Risk Assessments Deliver a Competitive Advantage

People who may believe this is simply about ticking a box off the DOJ list are missing the real value of conducting a risk assessment. Done

---

37   Aisling O'Shea et al., "DOJ Updates Guidance on the Evaluation of Corporate Compliance Programs," The Harvard Law School Forum on Corporate Governance, June 20, 2020, https://corpgov.law.harvard. edu/2020/06/20/doj-updates-guidance-on-the-evaluation-of-corporate-compliance-programs/.

properly, a compliance risk assessment will help you gain powerful knowledge about your unique mix of business risks and circumstances and deliver a decisive competitive advantage. How? With knowledge comes power—the power to compete and win aggressively by knowing what risks to avoid and how.

When conducting a risk assessment, you must dig deep into understanding your business first—your therapeutic areas of focus, from patient classes to type of disease and beyond—to help you uncover your greatest current strengths and uncover any perceived gaps. Companies making assumptions about any of this information are prone to bias and dangerous blind spots. These cannot only increase risk but also obscure valuable latent assets and advantages.

By thoroughly evaluating your current state of risks with a detailed assessment, ideally using an experienced and respected independent compliance expert, you gain crucial, credible, and valuable insight into your operations. At its core, an effective compliance risk assessment delivers the peace of mind and confidence you and your commercial team need to compete aggressively to win in the marketplace.

A compliance risk assessment is less painful, faster, and more affordable than you may think. Common misconceptions among life science companies include that compliance risk assessments are time consuming, expensive, and a hassle. It should take about sixty to ninety days to complete a comprehensive, customized evaluation and generate a detailed custom report, heat map of risks, and a detailed compliance implementation plan with minimal intrusion into the busy schedules of your employees. It can also build trust and confidence in the process with each interaction.

By bringing objective, targeted analysis that identifies any under- or overestimation of internal compliance processes in place and external compliance enforcement risks, you can identify any internal perception gaps and vulnerabilities and then map out analytics-based strategies and solutions. Above all, a risk assessment can help you understand what best practices and "success" look like *for you*. The goal is to minimize your compliance exposure to maximize your competitive edge.

As the Phillips Academy seal states, "Finis Origine Pendent"—"the end depends on the beginning." Start your company and compliance journey with a credible, effective risk assessment, and you will conclude your journey with success.

THE FUTURE LOOKS BRIGHT

My message to everyone is that it is not outdated to be a good, ethical, or law-abiding citizen who genuinely believes that most people, in their heart of hearts, are good. If you are indeed such an optimist, as I am, you will be successful and unleash energies that you may not have otherwise realized. Seeing this energy in action for myself working with companies and organizations whether in the world of corporate business, the military, politics, or athletics, it is all about tapping into your inner self to inspire others to a cause greater than yourself.

My hope is that through my words and actions, I will inspire others, in the spirit of Teddy Roosevelt, to "take the next step." Every day is a new day, and with that attitude, the sky is the limit.

CONCLUSION:

FIND YOUR INSPIRATION TO INSPIRE OTHERS

Leadership is all about people. It is not about organizations. It is not about plans. It is not about strategies. It is all about people—motivating people to get the job done. You have to be people centered.

—COLIN POWELL

agree with General Powell. It's about people. A large part of this book has been devoted to how we harness that recognition and bring to bear the human factors of rationality and emotion to inspire other people to be honest, to have integrity, to want to comply not for compliance's sake but in pursuit of a greater good bigger than any individual (i.e., to win with compliance and to propel performance).

As I have shared, I spent much of my life trying to live the values and principles taught to me by my parents, teachers, coaches, military, political, legal, and business leaders. But as I traveled on my life journey, I have come to appreciate the true importance and significance of these values and principles only recently after the kind of deep self-exploration that only comes from a "dark night of the soul"—in my case, a life-or-death struggle against COVID 19.

At the time, in late March and early April 2020, I was unsure if I would ever leave the hospital. For three days, Harvard-trained physicians, one a professor at Harvard Medical School and the other his student and resident assistant, told me in no uncertain terms, "Mr. Vincze, we don't know how this will end for you." In fact, those were their very first words to me when they came to see me in my hospital room in Beth Israel Hospital. Think about that for a moment. Let that sink in. These are among the best and brightest doctors in the world … and they "don't know." If they don't know, who does? At first, I tried to deflect this foreboding message with humor, responding to the doctors' grim greeting by saying, "Nice to meet you too, Doctor!" But there was no response, not a word, not a smile. Just a grim face staring at me and the monitors behind me.

Not until I was alone at night in my dark hospital room, hearing the screaming of an elderly lady in the room next to me, did I fully realize what I was facing—death. Even then, to my family, friends, and clients, I put on the "tough Marine" facade, posting on Facebook, "This Marine has only begun to fight and won't finish until he kicks COVID's butt!" I actually did this mostly for my daughter who was only eight at the time. But I did it, truth be told, for me as well.

For me the answer to the question, "If these doctors don't know how 'this will end' for me, who does?" became clear on the second night. It had now become like clockwork—waking up at 2:00 a.m.

gasping for air, barely able to breathe and not knowing if I would wake to see another day. This went on for several days and led to my admission to the hospital. As I lay there, not knowing if I would live or die and feeling an eerie sense of impending doom that this night would be the deciding night, I realized the only one who truly knew, who could possibly know for sure "how this will end," was God.

Now I am a very private person when it comes to religion. Raised a Roman Catholic and a graduate of St. Mary's Grammar School in Melrose, I had been an altar boy, and my eighth-grade teacher, Sister Mary Elizabeth, tried to convince me to become a priest, to forego attending Andover and enroll in the seminary. I told her I could not do that "because I liked girls too much and priests can't do that." She turned bright red and never mentioned it to me again! In retrospect, first, I was clearly correct about myself and why I could not be a priest. But I have often thought that being an ethics and compliance officer is a bit like being a secular corporate priest, encouraging people to do what's right, to be honest, and to be people of integrity. So maybe Sister Mary Elizabeth wasn't that far off after all.

But I was not a strict practicing Catholic, though I enjoyed going to church. Rather, I was a privately religious person who believed in God, the Ten Commandments, and a greater good and prayed almost every night silently before going to sleep. I had detected over the course of my life that whenever I prayed for anything for myself, those prayers generally went unanswered. The clearest example for me was that in high school, as a very strong athlete, I set some school weightlifting records for my age and weight. But I was only five feet eight inches, and I was convinced that if I could just get to six feet, then I would have the necessary height to be a world-class athlete. My goal was going to the Olympics on the US National Team in rowing. (I actually received an invitation to try out for the US National Team in college from my coach, who was a member of the team and a coach for the1980 team. As it turned out, that was the year President Carter boycotted the Moscow Olympics. So five feet eight inches or six feet, either way, it appears this was not meant to be!) I prayed and prayed and prayed on my knees ... and well ... nothing. I'm now five feet seven inches! (I've actually gotten shorter. Clearly, the prayers fell on deaf ears!) But on other occasions, for example, when it appeared that one of my friends from college was missing and in danger, I prayed for their safety and well-being, and then those prayers thankfully were indeed miraculously granted. So to me, the message from above was clear—be selfless in your prayers.

Fast-forward for a moment to today. Now that we are on the other side of the worst of the pandemic, it can be hard to remember just how vulnerable and uncertain—and downright scary—those times were. However, though I would never, ever wish such a personally devastating illness on anyone, the one silver lining was it truly afforded me a unique, life-changing opportunity to look into my own soul and conduct a real, raw, and honest assessment of who I am and what I truly believe in—as if my life depended on it ... because, as it turned out ... it did. The phrase "my life flashed before my eyes" is candidly spot-on.

Going back now to that dark night at 2:00 a.m. struggling to breathe, first, obviously, I thought of my family—my wife and young daughter. I had no intention of leaving my daughter fatherless before she was even out of elementary school! As I lay there, struggling to breathe, hooked up to IVs and oxygen and hearing the beeps of machines, I had a sudden epiphany, a crystal clear realization of what the truth was for me and what I had to do if, in fact, my death was imminent. I had to ask God for forgiveness of my sins and selflessly ask him to help not me but my family and especially my little girl. I prayed, "Dear Lord, if now is indeed the hour of my death and this is my time, and only you know if that is true, then I accept your will and trust in you. All I ask is that you watch over my family and especially my little girl. While I believe she truly needs me as her father to help her grow up, if that is not your will, then so be it. I entrust my soul and the well-being of my family unto you. P.S., I really think Chiara needs me as her dad!" I couldn't resist adding that final P.S. as life had taught me—you don't know until you ask—and I thought, "Why not? All He can say is no." But as soon as I finished uttering these words to myself, I remember being engulfed in a powerful sense of calm and tranquility and a deep feeling of inner peace. I had been true to my inner self of what I believed to be my duty, my truth. My thoughts were of the images we learned at parochial school with Jesus on the cross turning to heaven and saying to God the Father, *"Father, into thy hands I commend my spirit"* (Luke 23:46). And so I fell into a deep sleep.

The next morning, when I awoke, I honestly was unsure if I was indeed alive. I literally pinched myself to make sure I wasn't dreaming. I had had some very strange dreams the day before that seemed very real and verged on hallucinations, something other COVID-19 patients have been reported to have had. Yes, I was indeed alive! But the best was yet to be revealed. The doctor came in that afternoon and for the first time smiled and said my oxygen levels had improved significantly and felt I had turned a major corner in my fight with COVID-19. He cautiously shared that his experience with other COVID-19 patients was that once this happened, patients improved rapidly. I confided that I had given him and his resident assistant the names "Dr. Death and Dr. Doom" and had felt that Harvard had neglected their bedside manner training. He chuckled and offered to buy me pizza. I politely declined. Sure enough, he turned out to be right, and I was home by that weekend, with what turned out to be a still long recovery ahead.

Like for so many others, surviving this near-death experience was a life-changing event. It really changed me and inspired me in many ways, not the least of which was to write this book! I realized that life was very fragile and could be gone in an instant. I felt an obligation to "Earn this!" as Tom Hanks, playing the dying army captain and Ranger John Miller exhorted Private Ryan (played by Matt Damon) with his dying breath in the epic World War II movie *Saving Private Ryan* (1999). Yes, I was alive, and many others sadly were not. I had a new opportunity to make a difference in the world. To be selfless and to be true to the words "non sibi" (not for self) that appear in the Phillips Academy Seal.

Indeed, I had to "Earn this!" Now more than ever, I needed to live up to the standards, values, and principles with which I was raised and educated.

As I reflect on the principles of leadership I have emphasized in this book, and look for the most meaningful way to conclude in a way that may inspire you and other readers, two leaders in my life who inspired me come to mind: Gen. Colin Powell, US Army (ret.) and Lt. Gen. John F. Sattler, USMC (ret.).

I had the honor and privilege of working with both men, both great leaders.

Colin Powell rose from a humble beginning to the highest levels of military and political leadership, serving as a general in the US Army, as Chairman of the Joint Chiefs of Staff, as national security advisor to a president, and as Secretary of State. He used what God gave him, worked hard, exhibited integrity, and cared about his troops. As an effective leader, he earned the trust and respect of the people he served and of the people he led. He was genuine, authentic, and achieved results. By doing so, he inspired the people around him. I know—I was one of them when I worked in the Pentagon in the Office of the Secretary of Defense. He certainly inspired me. He inspired me to be selfless and to be dedicated to a purpose greater than myself. He led by example.

I'd like to share a personal story that comes to mind. Every November 10th, the Marine Corps celebrates the Marine Corps birthday, the date of the founding of the Marine Corps at Tun Tavern, Philadelphia, on November 10, 1775. In 1991 I was invited to be one of two Marine Corps captains to host the Marine Corp birthday ceremony in the Pentagon. My job was to introduce the cake cutting ceremony, its tradition and significance, and the oldest and youngest Marines whom we would be honoring, who traditionally received the first two pieces of the Marine Corps birthday cake, a tradition intended to honor the past and the future of the Corps. I was proud to be selected. I conducted research, wrote, rewrote, practiced, and rehearsed my lines repeatedly. This was quite an honor. When the moment of truth arrived, I walked out on stage behind the podium, and looked out at the audience. There appeared to be about a hundred people present. But in the very front sitting in the center, I saw the Secretary of Defense, Dick Cheney, General Colin Powell, Chairman of the Joint Chiefs of Staff, and what appeared to be every senior military officer from every branch of the service in the Pentagon. Behind me sat the Secretary of the Navy, the Commandant of the Marine Corps, and the oldest and youngest Marines whom we were about to recognize.

Captain Vincze,

Happy Birthday and Warm Regards.

Sean O'K...
Secretary of the Navy

*L. Stephan Vincze at Marine Corps birthday ceremony with Secretary
of the Navy Sean O'Keefe at the Pentagon on November 10, 1991*

Before breaking the silence and beginning my speech, the magnitude of the moment hit me. In true Hungarian fashion, I said to myself, "Vincze, don't fuck up now!" I chuckled to myself, took a deep breath, and confidently executed my mission. I knew that I was prepared and had the confidence from that preparation. Everything went perfectly. As the ceremony drew to a close, I looked back out at the audience. I saw General Powell looking at me. He simply smiled and nodded as if to say "Good job, Marine." That small gesture of appreciation meant a lot to me. He didn't have to do that, yet he did. I have never forgotten that and try to exhibit the same consideration to others who may be looking for my approval as a trusted leader. Sometimes, the smallest things in life may mean the most. He later signed his official portrait for me when I left the Pentagon to serve on Capitol Hill in May 1993.

I came to know Lt. Gen. John Sattler, USMC (ret.) on Capitol Hill, when he served as the Marine Corps congressional liaison officer to the US House of Representatives. At the time he was a lieutenant colonel who shortly thereafter was promoted to colonel. I had just arrived from the Pentagon. It was May 1993.

General Sattler is the most energetic person I have ever met in my life. Positive energy emanates from every pore. He is the personification of a leader who inspires and motivates others. That is why he later became a lieutenant general and the commanding officer of the I Marine Expeditionary Force during the war in Iraq in 2004, leading the battle of Fallujah, described as one of the fiercest, toughest battles of the entire Iraqi war. Later, General Sattler was assigned as the Commanding Officer of US Marine Forces Central Command and then as Director for Strategic Plans and Policy, Joint Staff on September 1, 2006. Lieutenant General Sattler retired effective August 1, 2008.

Capt. Vincze's promotion to Major Vincze with then-colonel John Sattler, USMC

Lieutenant General Sattler, USMC (ret.) also held the distinguished chair of leadership at the Stockdale Center for Ethical Leadership, located at the United States Naval Academy and more recently has been a motivational speaker, speaking on the importance of trust for innovation.

I am fortunate to have experienced the leadership of men like Colin Powell and John Sattler. These men not only led with their minds; they also led with their hearts, their passion. I felt their energy, their commitment, and yes, their integrity. You know it when you see it; you know it when you feel it. Similar to musical artists explaining that the secret to their creative talent is that "You have to feel the music," let me suggest that as effective leaders you need to engage your passion to allow your audience to feel your integrity. You supercharge your message by allowing your sincere passion for your work, your mission, and your vision to come through with what you say and how you say it, through what you do and how you do it. Effective artists connect with our souls. So do effective leaders. Generals Powell and Sattler connected with their troops as men, as leaders, as fellow human beings. They connected with me. I felt their energy, their passion, and their integrity. It inspired me to want to perform at my very best. I did not want to let these great

leaders down. This is what you need to do to inspire integrity. Once you do, compliance and performance follow.

This is how you win in life. This is how you win with compliance and propel performance.

So what does winning mean in this context? There is a greater good to which you are trying to contribute. Winning with compliance is tied to something greater than yourself; it is about a greater cause, a greater purpose. As a leader, part of your job is to convey that—to tie the vision of the product with the vision of the "moon shot"—the disease you are trying to cure, the lives you are trying to make better, healthier, easier.

The world you are trying to make better.

Compliance, as I have said throughout, does not usually put people at ease. But when you tie compliance to integrity, when you can inspire an organization to follow the North Star, compliance is suddenly the rocket fuel that will get you to that landing, to the prize.

Inspiration, integrity, ethics, compliance—they are the essential elements that will take your company to the heights of success. It is my hope that this book has inspired you to look and think about compliance differently and to be inspired to inspire others in pursuit of your vision of how to make our world a better place.

Kondracke: How House Moderates Pushed Clinton to Center, p. 7

ROLL CALL

THE NEWSPAPER OF CAPITOL HILL

VOL. 38, NO. 59   MONDAY, MAY 31, 1993 $2.50

Ten Hut! Former Marine Gets Top Committee Post

Pennsylvania Rep. Bill Clinger (R), ranking member of the House Government Operations Committee, has appointed a former U.S. Marine to the post of senior defense counsel on the panel's minority staff.

Steve Vincze, who was honorably discharged from the Marines just over a week ago after rising to the rank of major in April, will handle a number of defense and security-related duties in his new post.

For the last three years, Vincze was assigned to the office of the assistant secretary of defense for force management and personnel. In that post, he served as the Marine Corps representative and in-house counsel on transition and force-reduction issues with direct impact on service members, especially concerning separation and health benefits.

Before that posting, he was assigned to the office of the staff judge advocate at the Marine Corps Recruit Depot at Parris Island, S.C. Prior to getting his law degree, Vincze was assigned to the 1st Marine Division at Camp Pendleton, Calif., where he served as an artillery officer.

Upon his discharge, Vincze, a native of Centreville, Va., was awarded the Defense Meritorious Service Medal by the Department of Defense.

Vincze earned his bachelor's degree from Columbia University in 1982 and his law degree from Southern Methodist University School of Law in 1988. He is currently working towards his master of laws in international and comparative law at Georgetown University Law Center.

Former Marine Steve Vincze is the new senior defense counsel on the Government Operations minority staff.

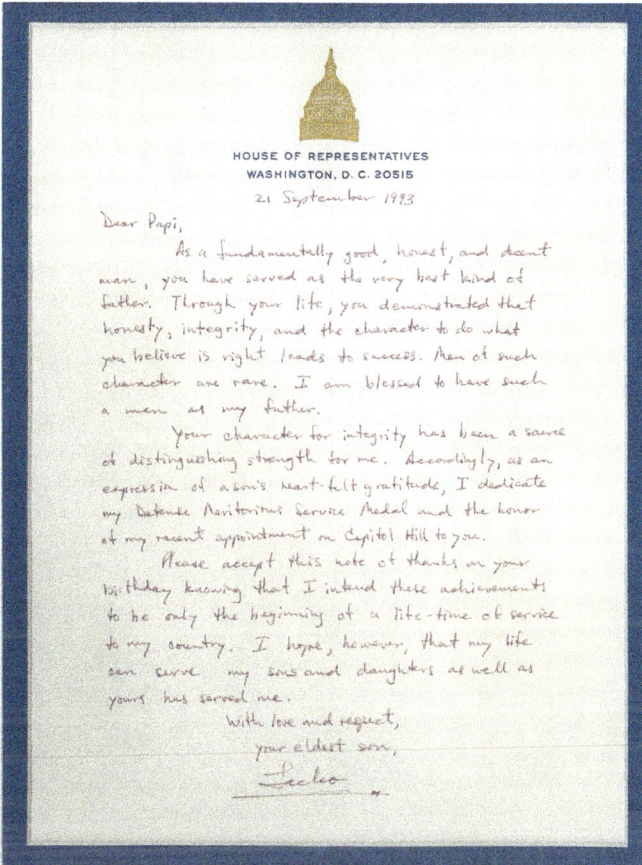

HOUSE OF REPRESENTATIVES
WASHINGTON, D.C. 20515

21 September 1993

Dear Papi,

As a fundamentally good, honest, and decent man, you have served as the very best kind of father. Through your life, you demonstrated that honesty, integrity, and the character to do what you believe is right leads to success. Men of such character are rare. I am blessed to have such a man as my father.

Your character for integrity has been a source of distinguishing strength for me. Accordingly, as an expression of a son's heart-felt gratitude, I dedicate my Defense Meritorious Service Medal and the honor of my recent appointment on Capitol Hill to you.

Please accept this note of thanks on your birthday knowing that I intend these achievements to be only the beginning of a life-time of service to my country. I hope, however, that my life can serve my sons and daughters as well as yours has served me.

With love and respect,
your eldest son,
Steve

Article clippings of L. Stephan Vincze's appointment as senior defense counsel, including the medal and Steve's letter to his father where he wrote about his father's integrity.

ABOUT THE AUTHOR

https://www.linkedin.com/in/stevevincze/

L. Stephan Vincze, JD, LLM, MBA

Prior to forming TRESTLE Compliance, LLC., Steve split his private sector career between service as an in-house or outsourced senior VP or VP chief compliance and privacy officer for several life science and healthcare companies and as a consultant, forming his own firms, as well as serving as a nonequity partner for a Big Four firm. A former counsel to a US House of Representatives Oversight Committee, he has nearly thirty years of experience in regulatory compliance matters, from government policy and enforcement to private sector business implementation considerations.

The real "Marine of Compliance," Steve has been recruited to address high-profile cases starting with the TAP case in 2001, which for many years was the largest settlement in the pharmaceutical industry, and to support legal, commercial, and executive teams and boards of directors with his compliance expertise. He has worked with a range of life science companies globally, including the very largest and most prominent US, Japanese, and European companies.

As a decorated officer in the US Marine Corps (USMC), Steve served as an artillery officer; received a full scholarship to law school; served as a prosecutor and defense counsel; served in the Office of the Secretary of Defense in the Pentagon, where he was awarded the Defense Meritorious Service Medal for his exemplary service; served as a reserve intelligence officer trained as a Defense Attaché to Hungary; and was recommended to serve as a counsel and professional staff member of the Government Operations Committee in the US House of Representatives. Steve has received several professional awards and recognitions to include Marquis' Who's Who in America and as a Top Business Professional. Steve is an internationally recognized speaker, author, and expert on ethics and compliance programs; he has been a guest lecturer at the University of Chicago, Harvard, UC Berkeley, University of Miami School of Business, INSEAD, and conferences around the world.

Steve attended Phillips Academy, Andover, and earned an AB from Columbia College, Columbia University, a JD from the Southern Methodist School of Law, an LLM in International and Comparative Law with distinction from the Georgetown University Law Center, and an MBA from the University of Chicago Graduate School of Business.

For more information on Steve and his company, TRESTLE Compliance, LLC, please visit https://www.linkedin.com/in/stevevincze/ and https://trestlecompliance.com/about/.

www.ingramcontent.com/pod-product-compliance
Lightning Source LLC
Chambersburg PA
CBHW071545200326
41519CB00021BB/6625